Business Writing Tips

For Easy and Effective Results

Robert Bullard

Published by Perfect Text, Oxford
www.perfecttext.org

ISBN: 978-0-9931898-0-7

Typeset by Fakenham Prepress Solutions, Fakenham, Norfolk NR21 8NN

To: Oxfordshire County Council Library Services

With thanks for all your wonderful resources (in particular Oxford Central Library) and endlessly helpful counter staff.

Contents

Contents

Acknowledgements

My thanks to Tom Hardy, of Tom Hardy Publishing (for comments on my draft), Fakenham Prepress (typesetting), Nikki Shield, of Designs Like These (cover design) and Sophie Collins (proofreading).

Preface

Writing Skills Can Be Learnt!

Writing is not easy – or not always. Finding the right words, deciding their best order, making them grab the reader, and polishing your text, can all be surprisingly hard work. What is more, it's probably a long time since most of us were at school or college, which is the last time most us ever got any formal help with our writing.

However, as a trainer in writing skills, I know that writing skills *can be learnt*. And as a trainer, there is nothing I enjoy more than sharing my knowledge with others and helping people improve their writing, so that they can achieve their goals. Those are my aims of this book.

The 17 chapters cover the everyday writing needs where – from my experience as a trainer, copywriter, copy-editor and proofreader – people most often ask for help or need inspiration. Each chapter has ten tips that will bring you quick and effective results, along with ideas for further reading, and writing exercises, to expand and consolidate your learning. And throughout the book there are examples of good writing, insightful quotes from authors and 'Key Points'.

You will find chapters/parts on topics such as: How to write with ease and speed (Chapter 2), Grab your readers' attention (Chapter 6), Ways to make your writing memorable (Chapter 8), Writing for particular outputs – such as websites, reports and press releases (Chapters 10–13) and Tidying your text (Chapters 14–16). But those are just examples; a complete list of contents is available.

And finally, my tips are applicable to *anyone* – whatever your position and wherever you work. You may be a manager, project staff or working in PR or communications. You may be in an SME or a FTSE 100. And you may be in the public, private or third sector. All that matters is you write as part of your job, and are looking for help, tips and ideas.

Before You Start Writing

What makes writing hard?

It starts with the keyboard/pen

Anxieties creep in

The format for school/college writing is wrong for business

We try and write like someone else

We think our writing needs to be 'perfect'

Grocers don't help

Writing takes *so long*!

We don't get any training

Receiving feedback isn't easy

People don't *have* to read your work

66 Writing is the hardest work in the world not involving heavy lifting. 99

Pete Hamill (US Journalist)

There is no doubt about it, writing can be hard work. I know from my own experience: as a journalist, from training people in writing skills and book coaching, and from seeing what authors have to go through to produce a book.

However, I firmly believe that writing skills *can be taught*. You may not be the next J.K. Rowling (or you may!) but there is no reason why your writing can't improve, and become good. Like any other skill, it just takes guidance, study and practice.

For anyone who finds writing hard work, this chapter is especially for you. You may have had a poor education, not written much of length since school/college, or maybe writing was never your greatest strength. I suggest some of the reasons you may struggle, and have a few tips for getting those issues sorted. Read on.

It starts with the keyboard/pen

Talking is easy, we do it all the time and can do it pretty much without thinking. But how much time do we spend typing/writing? No wonder we are better at communicating with our mouths than with the keyboard/pen.

And while talking can be fast, and can be done without a second thought, writing is slower, which gives us time to think. Time to think. Along with a blank screen/page that means …

Anxieties creep in

You need to be fairly confident of what you are writing about. But here are three areas where you might worry, and that could affect your writing. Do any ring true?

- ◆ 'I was no good at English at school – I can't remember the grammar we were taught. I get some words muddled, and sometimes spell things wrongly. I am nervous of showing myself up to others.'

◆ 'I don't know enough about what I am writing – I don't have all the facts/information I need. What if there are any errors in it, if experienced people see it, and have already said it?'

◆ 'I don't have enough time – My deadline is imminent. I don't have enough time to do the research, and to do a proper job.'

Each of these also make writing harder. But if you put aside your inner critic, find yourself a 'voice', and just keep writing (more on these methods in Chapters 2, 4 and 5), you will be on the road to achieving your writing goals.

The format for school/college writing is wrong for business

At school and college we were taught to follow a very precise structure for our essays. It would be something like: Introduction – Aims – Methodology – Results – Discussion – Conclusions. However, that is usually the wrong structure for business writing, which often puts the conclusions or benefits *first* (see Chapters 6, 10 and 13).

Another thing wrong with school writing was that we believed that anything longer was automatically better: it could mean a few extra marks. Indeed, we may have got used to writing waffle (or long sentences rather than concise ones) as a way to get closer to our teacher's suggested page length/word count. Again, this is not good practice for good business writing, which emphasises the need to be concise and precise.

And finally, the grammatical rules we were taught at school: like never split an infinitive, you can't start sentences with 'And' or 'But', and conjunctions replace the need for commas. Well, these served us well as children, but since then language and conventions have changed. For more on this, see Chapters 14 and 15; but if you doubt me, just look at this advice from the Plain English Campaign – what better authority than them?

Dispelling grammatical myths

We're not trying to be trendy here by breaking grammatical rules. We're just going to destroy some of the grammatical myths.

◆ You can start a sentence with and, but, because, so or however.

◆ You can split infinitives. So you can say to boldly go.

◆ You can end a sentence with a preposition. In fact, it is something we should stand up for.

◆ And you can use the same word twice in a sentence if you can't find a better word.

Of course, this does not mean you should break these so-called rules all the time – just when they make a sentence flow better.

SOURCE: Extract from *How to Write Plain English* – Plain English Campaign.

We try and write like someone else

As a result of the pressures above some of us approach writing as though it requires a different language to speaking, which of course it doesn't. These tendencies are quite common, but should be avoided:

◆ To make our writing 'sound good' we use unusual words, plus long-winded and sophisticated phrases. (*Endeavour* instead of *try*, *aforementioned* instead of *previous*, etc.)

◆ Our writing becomes overly formal, using words and phrases we wouldn't write or normally speak.

◆ In order 'to fit in' we consciously or unconsciously adopt the writing style of where we work, or the writing style of the occupation we are trying to be. (Do solicitors come to mind?!) We don't question whether the style is clear and appropriate for the audience.

◆ As a result, we lose our 'natural voice' (i.e. what your writing sounds like because of the words you use, your content and writing style, etc.).

As hinted in the final point, we should write in the way that is true to ourselves, with our natural voice coming off the page. My advice is use a relaxed, everyday language, and don't try and be anyone else. Good writing is sometimes described as though you were speaking on the page. Or in the words of Somerset Maugham: 'Good prose should resemble the conversation of a well-bred man.'

We think our writing needs to be 'perfect'

Many people say to me 'I can't write', but on discussion it is clear that their problem is actually something else. Because we put authors on a bit of pedestal, we fear our writing has to attain that higher level – it even has to be *'perfect'*. But we are not trying to write best-sellers, merely to be clear and grammatically correct. Could that issue be holding you back?

I notice this in particular when running training courses in how to write a blog. Delegates are often fearful of publishing any of their practice exercises on their blog – even if they can edit them later or delete them at the touch of a button (and, I'm sorry, but there is virtually no chance of anyone actually seeing or reading them!).

Grocers don't help

Even if people make mistakes, they can still communicate in their writing. The 'grocer's apostrophe' is a perfect example of this, where market stallholders (traditionally grocers) sometimes put apostrophes in the wrong place on their signs, e.g. *Tomatoes' £84p/lb*. And because no one corrects their mistakes, and some people are unsure or think the grocers are/may be right, it dents people's confidence (has the grocer got that apostrophe right?) and the mistakes spread through society.

In the same way, we absorb and follow the bad writing practices of the world around us. Overly long sentences, the use of jargon and waffle and incorrect punctuation, etc. can all creep into our writing, almost without us noticing. *So be alert as you write and edit your work.*

Writing takes *so long*!

Some people get frustrated that they can't get their words right the first time around. They make mistakes or think of better ways to say things, and as a result have to edit their text again and again and again.

If this applies to you, don't be dispirited. Revising and editing is a normal part of writing. Honest. (Just look at the number of changes, corrections and re-workings in the writings of any author, in their draft manuscripts.) It is only when you *really* know a subject, and/or are writing full time, that you will get things right at the first attempt.

Yes, writing might seem simple enough compared to some of the other skills you have mastered (after all, it only requires 'picking up a pen'), but saying what you want, putting the words in the right order, making sure they sound good and are grammatically correct, and flow on from what came before, isn't easy. Regrettably, it doesn't happen automatically.

We don't get any training

For most of us, we probably had our last lesson or training in how to write when at school/college. Which was probably a long time ago. And anyway, that was for a different kind of writing. But have you had any training in writing skills *since*? Great if you did, but it's very likely that you didn't.

And yet if business reports are important, if marketing material is to work the wonders expected of it, and if a website is to improve a company's performance in line with mangers' expectations, shouldn't there be more training in how to write?

Just because we can pick up a pen and communicate, doesn't mean we can't learn from a course in how to write more effectively, and for particular outputs and audiences.

Receiving feedback isn't easy

Receiving feedback isn't easy if we have spent ages working on a document, are now emotionally attached to it, and as a result are defensive about its content and conclusions. And especially if the feedback is quite critical, and poorly given.

However, getting feedback is essential as, because we write alone, we can get too close to our document. For example, in collating different material and pooling several people's comments we may miss the bigger questions of whether the document's overall structure and format are appropriate. And, when editing and revising something we can become so familiar with the text that we read *what we think or meant to be there* rather than spotting the typos etc. *that are there.*

So, you must get feedback on your writing from others – before you distribute/publish it. Whatever you do, don't be tempted to go it alone. However unpleasant the feedback pill might be, think how much worse the experience would be if any of your mistakes were shared with a wider audience.

People don't *have* to read your work

Have you ever read a *bad* novel? One that was badly written, whose story didn't grip you or you didn't care what happened in the end? It may sound odd but, surprisingly, most of us have.

The reason we continue reading such books – sometimes to the end and even without skimming – is usually because we have some kind of emotional or financial commitment to it, i.e. we were given it, bought it, liked the author's last book, it passes the time while we are commuting/travelling, or we are on holiday and have nothing else to read.

Sadly, *your* readers won't have that same commitment. You can't bank on them to read to the end. Faced with bad business writing – a poor writing style, inappropriate content, lack of clarity, etc. – they will opt out. And they probably won't come back. Ever.

So, whether you are writing a website, brochure, marketing letter, report, whatever, it is essential that you write well, to keep your target audience reading. And don't just write well, you need to engage them with the right kind of language, answer their questions, deal with their concerns, etc. – topics I deal with in the following chapters.

Practice writing exercises

Make a list of the anything you find hard about writing – that you are fearful of, that stops you writing, makes it hard work, etc. Alongside each one, make a note of my suggestions for resolving the issue in this chapter, Chapters 2 and 7 – or on the web. Keep the notes as support for the next time you have to do some writing.

Find some writing that you enjoy reading – it might be a book, newspaper, magazine, etc. Re-read it, trying to identify what parts you like, i.e. is it the language, description, characters, plot, dialogue, etc.? Read more by this author; you will be surprised how much of their style you absorb in your writing.

Are there any aspects of your writing that you think you need to work at, e.g. do you use overly long sentences, or are you unsure of your paragraphing, grammar or punctuation? The relevant chapters/parts in this book should help, or a book from the library, a day's training, etc. Email me if you need advice: robert@perfecttext.org. A bit of guidance and a bit of practice should help you sort them out.

On the web, do a search for 'original book manuscript'. Notice how much some of these documents were edited by their authors prior to publication – and these are probably *the later drafts*. As a guide, I suggest that, together, editing and proofreading will take you around 25–40 per cent of the total time you spend working on a job.

2

How to write with ease and speed

Don't start too early

No need to start at the beginning

Check you know your audience and objectives

Plan what you are going to write

Look for a strong thread, or story

Use everyday language

WRITE, don't edit

Push yourself

Thought you learnt *the opposite* at school?

If you get stuck...

❝ There is nothing to writing. All you do is sit down at a typewriter and bleed. **❞**

Ernest Hemingway

If you've just read the last chapter, all is not lost. This book gives you the tips for writing effectively in the business world and first up is how to write a bit more 'effortlessly' – with ease and speed.

Don't start too early

When we have a job to do, any job, it is tempting to feel it's better to get started as soon as possible – after all, with the wheels turning we'll finish sooner. And if the job is a new one, exciting or pressing, the temptation to start before you are fully ready is even greater. But my advice is *don't*.

As anyone who has done any DIY will know only too well, the lack of sound planning and preparation before you start usually means having to redo what you did first – and worse still, a 'botch job'. Or it is like choosing to cook something new without having fully read the recipe beforehand – so you discover half-way through that you are missing a key ingredient, or don't have enough time for it to cook, etc.

Also, a lot of writing requires you to go through an 'incubation period' first, as you mull over e.g. how to start your text, how the different sections will fit together, what's the best way to say things, etc.

If you start writing *without* thinking through your document's objectives, who is the audience, and without a plan for your content, etc., you are likely to regret it. At the very least it will probably require a lot of editing as you make it more like what you *had meant to write* – worse, you could miss your objectives completely. Endless editing can also knock your confidence.

> **Key Point:** So, don't pick up your pen until you have reminded yourself what and why you are writing, for whom, and how you are going to say it.

No need to start at the beginning

Beginnings are important – be they to brochures, marketing letters, blogs or whatever. They need to be just right. But they are the not always the right place to start writing. This might sound strange but, if you are writing anything more than a page, until you have written the rest/the majority, you won't know how (or how best) to begin your document. And knowing it needs to be 'just right' will just put pressure on your writing – and could even tie you up in knots.

> **Key Point:** My advice is to start writing your document at a part that is easy, and only return to writing the beginning when you can see how best to introduce the rest.

Check you know your audience and objectives

Think for a moment how you talk differently to: your partner, work colleague, close friend, family member, shop assistant and a total stranger. In the same way we adjust how we *speak* in these situations, we should adjust our *writing* according to our audience. And that means having a good idea of who they are.

Magazines have a very good idea of their audience, which they develop into 'readership profiles' that outline their typical reader's gender, age range, type of occupation, education, income, lifestyle, etc. An example of a readership profile is given below, but you will find more, and different types, on the web.

Having a profile like this helps their journalists/contributors stay reminded of their readers as they write: the language they should use, the sorts of issues readers are interested in and their wants from the magazine, etc. (Just think how different the readers will be, for example, of *Motorcycle News* and *Sainsbury's Magazine*.) So, if you don't know your audience it is time to do some market research.

Example of a readership profile

Professional Driver is the only magazine dedicated to the private hire and chauffeur sectors. Our monthly mix of news, features, road tests and

---

business advice makes Professional Driver an essential read for anybody in this vibrant and growing business – from one-man operators to large private hire and chauffeur fleets.

The sector has continued to thrive, and employs around 200,000 people in the UK. It is becoming an increasingly sophisticated business, and Professional Driver is proud to play a leading role in providing our readers with the information they need to run their businesses to the highest standards of quality and customer service.

Professional Driver readers include large fleet directors and owner-driver operators, from the chauffeur, private hire and taxi sectors. Our controlled circulation readership means only named individuals within companies can receive copies of the magazine. This gives us access to detailed data about our readers and their job functions, ensuring a highly relevant, targeted circulation for advertisers … [then follows some statistical and other data on job, fleet size, buying decisions, type of car, etc.].

SOURCE: www.prodrivermags.com

As well as being reminded of your audience as you write, it is useful to have a reminder of your objectives. They only need to be scribbled down on a piece of paper, but keep this alongside you. Seeing them in front of you as you write will ensure you keep focussed on the job.

Plan what you are going to write

During my early days as a freelance journalist, when writing 800–2,500 word features for national newspapers, I spent far too long editing my work. Far far too long. Then one day, when attending a training course for new journalists, I realised why. Yes, I was getting commissions from editors. Yes, I was doing good supporting interviews and research. But I wasn't *planning* enough when it came to the writing. (Later, I was reminded of my schoolteachers' message prior to doing essay-writing exams: 'Read the question and *plan your answer.*')

How much you should plan your writing depends on the length of your document. Even if it is only short, I find it worth doing a quick sketch, to organise my thoughts. But for anything over 300 words, making a more detailed plan will help you:

◆ Work out the best way to order different sections, and see the possible links between them (some people find it very useful to *physically* move things around on a page, using cut-outs);

◆ Decide the right balance between the sections (i.e. how much to write on each);

◆ Spend less time editing.

Key Point: Many people find this technique useful. First, calculate how many words/pages your document needs to be. Then divide the total into the different sections you think the reader will expect to see covered in such a work, allocating a word/page count for each. Some sections may be straightforward, but longer ones may need sub-dividing. For example, a letter bidding for some work might have an Introduction (50 words), Summary/Close (100), Testimonials and Relevant experience (500), etc.

If you do this before you even start your research, and writing, it means you can make time-saving decisions beforehand. For example, you will know how many quotes and examples you can fit into 500 words, so won't collect more than you can fit. Then, as you write, keep an eye on your word/page count, so that you don't go much over the word/page count you allocated for each section. It's a simple tool, but excellent for ensuring you write with the shape of the end product in mind from the start.

Look for a strong thread, or story

As part of your plan above you should try and identify some 'links' between sequential paragraphs and sections, so that your document has a strong thread. So that it 'flows' naturally and readers want to read more, as opposed to it jumping around haphazardly and is hard to follow. The links may be similar ideas, a reference to the same person, or something they said, or something that happened at the same time (year/month/day), etc.

Maybe there is even a story, which can be very effective for engaging your reader. Everyone loves a story and even business writing can have a story to it. For example, Situation – But/Challenge – Solution – Problems – Readjustment – Finish – Outcome.

Tell a story to your readers

Business that stretched from ski lifts to face lifts

New Zealander Mel Braham was born in a household where business was part of everyday conversation – and it wasn't long before he was dreaming up money-making schemes of his own.

His father, originally from England, owned a fashion-manufacturing firm supplying department stores and had also set up a chain of shops. His mother invested in property, which she sold at a large profit.

By the age of 20, Braham was in business himself. Spotting a niche in the market for low-cost ski holidays, he set up a firm offering package deals for budget travellers.

By cheaply securing the winter lease on a logging camp owned by Wellington University in a popular skiing area of North Island, Braham undercut accommodation costs of all the country's ski companies. The firm grew rapidly, becoming New Zealand's largest ski-tour business. Two years later Braham moved to Australia where he set up a sister travel agency, with offices in Sydney, Brisbane and Melbourne.

COMMENTS: This column tells entrepreneurs' stories very well, so is worth reading. Particularly good is this piece's pace, which starts quickly and never slows. Each paragraph moves the story on, and by the third we have covered his family and why he is in business. Telling his background and his parents' activities puts some depth on him as a character, and creates a wider story. The key points are emphasised at the end of sentences ('making schemes of his own', 'large profit') and in short sentences ('By the age of 20, Braham was in business himself.') We are now only about one-fifth of the way through the whole piece (not shown here), and can tell from the title there is a lot more yet to come. By now most readers will be hooked.

SOURCE: 'How I Made It' column, *Sunday Times*

Use everyday language

If you don't write very often, don't have much knowledge of/experience in the subject, or worse still are worried you are *no good* at writing, your writing may become tense. You may use unusual words, and your style may become overly formal. If you think about it, we react the same when we find ourselves in uncomfortable social situations: we become tense and don't act/feel ourselves.

If this applies to your writing, be aware of it, and try to 'dress down'. I don't mean write in slang, or like youngsters talk on the street and on Social Media, but as though one of your readers was in front of you, and you were talking to them. The guidance for a good writing style is to write as clearly as we talk. If you do that you won't be far wrong. Hopefully this example from my blog fits the bill.

How this book happened

Apparently, when I was young I told people that when I grew up I wanted to be a lorry driver.

APPARENTLY.

Maybe it was because of my large dinky car collection, the time I spent playing with it, or that I did not know there were more exciting driving jobs.

However, what I do know is this…

I was brought up in a house filled with books and news-obsessed, and in my teens we lived in Germany. So, because I spoke virtually no German, a highlight of the day was when my father brought home the British newspapers – after they had been flown out from England (those were the days)! I loved kneeling on floor, poring over them; I loved meeting British journalists who were based in Germany; and I loved romanticising about a career as one of *them*…

SOURCE: From my blog, www.perfecttext.org/blog

WRITE, don't edit

Computers have made writing so easy, compared to writing by hand and using a typewriter. They have made it easier to write long documents, and to change things along the way. But neither of these are that helpful. First, length doesn't equate with success. Secondly, perennial editing takes you away from the real job: stopping and starting doesn't allow your writing to 'flow'; it focusses your mind on fine details rather than 'the bigger picture', and therefore hinders your overall progress.

> **Key Point:** In particular when you are starting out to write something, it is far better to do what people call 'free writing' – to allow your flow of thoughts to begin. That doesn't mean writing without a clear plan, but *without any editing*, which you can come back to later.

Push yourself

If you haven't done much writing for several years, and/or felt you were never that good at it, or didn't enjoy it, you may find it rather hard work – especially at the start. As a result, you may feel like taking a break or two, passing the job to someone else, or even giving up completely. I understand. At times, I too have felt 'not in the mood' to write. But my advice is that, if you persevere, you will surprise yourself. No, *starting* may not be that easy, especially getting past the first few paragraphs, hours or pages. But every additional sentence you write will get your creative juices going, making your next one that little bit easier.

> **Key Point:** Allocate at least two to three hours for each writing session, and don't allow yourself a break for at least an hour. That way you will have made some visible progress by the end, and feel OK about returning to it next time – and even look forward to it.

Thought you learnt *the opposite* at school?

When I do talks and give training in business writing skills people invariably ask me grammatical questions such as these three: 'Do you allow split infinitives?' (e.g. *To* boldly *go*); and 'Is it OK to start sentences with "And"?'

The reason they ask these questions is because their age and/or background means that they learnt Latin at school, or their teachers were brought up on Latin, and in Latin *you can't* split an infinitive, nor can you end a sentence with a preposition. As for 'and', it is a conjunction and conjunctions are for *joining* words and phrases, not starting them. So these three practices shouldn't be allowed, people tell me firmly. Or should they?

My answer? Well, I don't support the dropping of grammatical rules, and certainly not the introduction of textspeak from Social Media, but we have to acknowledge that language changes. First, Latin needn't be the base of our rules any more. And secondly, teachers simplified things for our benefit. For example, 'To boldly go where no man has gone before' is from Star Trek; and the third sentence of the Bible ('And God saw that the light was good ... '), and the fifth and eighth, all start with 'And ...'.

> **Key Point:** Don't get tangled up by out-of-date or oversimplified 'rules' from your schooldays: rules that we were taught for a reason at the time but needn't apply to your writing today. If you take a detailed look at some quality newspapers and magazines, I think you will be surprised.

If you get stuck...

We all get stuck when writing sometimes – we can't find the right word, can't find how best to compose a sentence, or can't see a way to link several ideas. So here are some tips to clear what is probably just a temporary blockage.

◆ Forget about the problem – you can come back to it later. For the moment, keep on writing.

◆ Speak the sentence or talk through your ideas out loud. You'll be amazed at how forcing yourself to *speak* can clear a blockage and produce the right words.

◆ Take a break. It needn't be long, but something that will take your mind off your writing. Do a job around the house, go shopping, or go for a short walk. They will clear your mind and help you sort things out on your return.

For more on overcoming writing challenges see Chapter 7.

Further reading

HBR Guide to Better Business Writing – Bryan A. Garner. Harvard Business Review Guides, 2012.

Perfect Text blog. Available at: www.perfecttext.org/blog/

The Plain English Campaign. Free guides. General guides – How to write plain English. Available at: www.plainenglish.co.uk/free-guides.html

Practice writing exercises

Write a letter to one of your school or college teachers, saying how they helped you, giving a brief history of what you have done since school/college, and saying you would like to meet up next holidays. Spend a few minutes planning your letter, write without taking any breaks, and make sure you have a really good beginning and ending. Then leave what you have written for a few hours/days. When you read it back to yourself, make a note of anything you felt was (a) good or (b) needed improvement, making the changes as needed. This exercise will take you through the stages of planning, writing and editing a piece of text for a comfortable, non-work task.

Repeat the task described above, but this time for a work-related letter/document.

Make a note of any 'rules' about writing that you firmly believe in (e.g. about starting sentences with 'and', splitting infinitives, the use of commas, etc.) from lessons you were taught at school, etc. Check to see if these 'rules' still hold today using my advice in Chapters 1 and

2, or what you can find out on the web. Email me if you need help: robert@perfecttext.org.

Plan and structure a piece of work-related writing as per my advice on p. 15. If you do this *before you start writing* it will significantly reduce the amount (and nature) of information you have to collect.

Part **2**

Putting Pen to Paper

3

Write for your audience

66 Your audience is one single reader. I have found that sometimes it helps to pick out one person – a real person you know, or an imagined person – and write to that one. 99

John Steinbeck

Don't forget your readers

One of the commonest mistakes of all that I encounter is people forgetting to think *who* they are writing for, and failing to write from that perspective (as opposed to their own). How come? Well, it is not that surprisingly when you think about. Day in, day out, we live and breathe our own organisations, sit within our own departmental structures, and think of things from our own perspective, etc. And as a result we write from this viewpoint, rather than our readers'. It's only normal.

A common example of this is organisations wanting to tell people about their company details (e.g. when they were formed, and what is their mission statement, etc.), whereas customers are far more interested in their *services* – and more specifically, can they solve their needs.

Here are three examples of company advertisements that I think engage well with their readers.

Catch your readers' interest

The Greyhound, Besslesleigh – We are a pub to the bottom of our boots, and have a real focus on good quality, fresh food which we source locally wherever possible. You won't find televisions, gaming machines or pool tables, but you will find a warm and chatty pub with lots of character.

COMMENTS: Straightforward prose ('We are a pub to the bottom of our boots') always works well with readers. Refreshing honesty, highlighting what the pub *doesn't have* as well as what it does, will appeal to its target customers. In addition, the strong descriptive image ('a warm and chatty pub with lots of character') gets their readers half way there – in their minds at least.

Barcote Park – WHY WE LOVE IT. Feel like the lord of the manor, the chance of a lifetime to live in this opulent Parkland setting. History, high ceilings, and the height of fashion, the management charge is low at £1,600 per year. Guide Price £700,000.

COMMENTS: In this short advert, Oxford estate agents Pink and Black use status and emotions ('lord of the manor' and 'opulent Parkland setting') to fire up potential housebuyers' interest. To nudge people to book a viewing, or call in, they also create a sense of urgency ('chance of a lifetime') and allay what might be some people's fears ('the management charge is low').

Le Creuset 25cm Oval Casserole Dish – Le Creuset is synonymous with high quality. The smooth enamel finish is durable and hygienic, meaning everything you stew, braise or simmer in a Le Creuset casserole will taste as good as you intended. It also means your dishes will look great on the hob, in the oven and on the table... Perfect for creating a variety of meals for one or side dishes for your meals. They are truly versatile and are perfect for marinating, baking, roasting, serving or simply storing.

COMMENTS: In my mind, powerful and persuasive writing from Le Creuset. The descriptive text takes the products from the printed page into readers' imagination ('smooth enamel finish', 'everything you stew, braise or simmer'). Claiming to do what every cook would like fulfils readers' dreams ('will taste as good as you intended', 'your dishes will look great'). Key messages are repeated ('perfect'), and putting things in threes creates a lovely punchy rhythm ('on the hob, in the oven and on the table'.)

SOURCE: Newspaper advertisements

Another mistake is to describe a company based on how it is structured (because that is how it operates and is organised) as opposed to thinking of *the services it provides*, which is what customers want to know.

It may sound like rather a subtle difference, but it will have major consequences on what you write.

What is your readers' background?

You should also think about the type of person you are writing for: their age, background, level of education, prior knowledge of the subject, disposable income, how much time they have, etc.

To do this, magazines draw up 'readership profiles' that they use to help secure advertising but also to guide anyone new to writing for them, so that their language, examples/case studies, and the issues they explore, etc. are as relevant and familiar to their readers as possible – otherwise people will stop reading. (Imagine how different the readers will be, for example, for magazines as diverse as *Community Care*, *Investors Chronicle* and *Quiltmaker Magazine*.)

As an aside, a publisher recounted to me recently how authors of school textbooks frequently have difficulty in remembering who they are writing for: the students or their teachers. For while textbooks are *read* by both, some authors are anxious for the teachers to think highly of their textbook, so have *teachers* in mind as their audience. But the proper audience for textbooks is *students*; authors must write textbooks addressed to *them*, not their teachers.

Key Point: You will find it helpful to draw up a readership profile of *your* audience (there is an example of one in Chapter 2) – and at the very least have a mental picture of your typical readers, using a friend/neighbour who fits the profile, or someone you make up in your mind from a collection of characteristics. It'll help your writing talk more to the reader.

Why are they interested?

Most documents are read for a particular purpose – even leaflets that are casually picked up only out of passing interest. But have you thought *why* the people might be reading your text: do they have to, or are they looking for something specific – and if so, what?

Thinking a little about your audience will help guide your writing, and here are a few things to think about:

- What stage of the buying process are they: are they just browsing, looking for information, or ready to buy?
- Do you need to include any particular buzz words to engage with them?
- What is their timescale: do they need something now, sometime soon, or in the future?
- Do you need to spell out the benefits of your products/services, and in how much detail?

Serve your readers on a plate

As part of the above, think what you can do to ensure your text is geared to your readers' needs as much as possible – serve things up for them on a plate.

So, instead of talking generally about how good your product/service is, put something like '*5 Reasons for Choosing us*', listing the reasons in a group. Instead of reproducing your testimonials, put them under a heading like '*Join our Rank of Super-happy Customers*'. And instead of trying to encourage people to support an initiative, advise them of the '*5 Benefits of Sponsorship*'.

Lists like these work wonderfully. They force you to crystallise things from the readers' perspective. They make maximum value of your information. And they are so much more powerful than burying your points within long paragraphs of text. (If you want further examples, take a look at high-street magazines, which have got particularly good at this.)

Tuning into readers' needs is sometimes paralleled with the actions of golfers as they prepare to hit a golf shot. In the same way that golfers size up the lie of the land in front of them – checking the distance, gradient, bumps, dips and the wind – so must you be on top of your readers' character, knowledge, preferences, needs, situation, etc.

Be careful with your jargon

We all work in our particular business/organisation niches, and within them we are all drowned by jargon, acronyms, and particular termi-nology. But we sometimes forget that the words and phrases which are so familiar to us, aren't to everyone.

So, when writing for the outsider make sure you challenge yourself as to whether your writing will be understood. Not just obvious things like spelling out acronyms the first time you use them, but using words that the man on the street will understand exactly what you mean.

Where are they reading your text?

I always think that a big factor in how, and whether or not, people respond to advertising material (brochures and leaflets as well as adverts) depends on *where* it is seen, and what it is positioned next to. So, think for a moment, are such issues relevant to you.

For example, if you are writing a webpage, remember that most people are likely to skim it rather than read it in full. In contrast, if you are writing something for a newspaper or magazine that readers have *paid for*, they are more likely to read all of your article. Other issues for you might be: are there any articles/documents surrounding yours that might influence the reader; will they be reading at work or at home; at what time of day, etc. All of these could affect your heading and introduction, your writing style, the language you use, content, etc.

An example of this is how, because people now get nearly all their messages over the computer – email, Social Media, the web, etc. – *old-fashioned approaches* by direct mail, or snail mail, can now really stand out and get people's attention. So it might be one method worth building into your next marketing campaign.

What do you want them to do as a result?

Before you start writing, be clear in your mind as to your objectives: what do you want readers to do as a result of reading your document. Do you want them to: contact you (and in which case is the phone number/ email clear); visit your website (have you written the web address, and is that the right webpage to take them to); complete and return a coupon (should you refer to it, rather than just including it, and what are they left with when they cut it out).

Readers may have reservations

Many people who pick up and read one of your brochures or leaflets, or come across your webpages, etc., will have concerns about some aspect of what you are offering. It may be your price (or their affordability of it), your terms and conditions, the time needed to do it, or that they have not done it/used one before and don't know anyone who has, etc.

Make sure you address these kinds of worries in your text. Can you give them a money-back guarantee; or can you offer them something extra (ideally that won't cost you anything but will seem like they are getting something for free, e.g. a 30-day refund, etc.). You need to reassure such people in whatever ways you can.

The value of testimonials

If you are writing sales literature, your target customers will be far more persuaded by the words and experiences of other customers, than by you. So, it is worth making a lot of effort to collect supportive testimonials and recommendations.

Sometimes people moan to me about the work involved in doing this, and how long it takes to get people's approval, etc. But remember, once such quotes are obtained they will help influence other sales, and can be used again and again, and in different places. Believe me, they will be worth the effort of collecting them; they won't disappoint.

Further reading

On Message – Theo Theobald. Kogan Page, 2013.

Practice writing exercises

Compare how a big news story (or a sports report) is covered in a tabloid versus a broadsheet newspaper. How would you describe the two writing styles, and what can you say about their different readerships. Now write an imaginary report for a sport of your choice, *for your audience*.

Describe what your business/organisation does (in 50–100 words) to these three audiences: (a) a new member of staff; (b) a journalist who covers your industry/sector; and (c) someone from your family. Before writing, decide what you will stress, how you will explain things, what wording you will use or avoid, etc.

Repeat the task above, but restricting your descriptions for each audience to just one sentence.

Collect some free literature that comes through your letterbox, or that you find in public places around where you live and work. See which ones immediately stand out as good, and then examine why. What techniques do they use, for example, to get readers' attention, get them to keep reading, deal with their possible reservations, and get people to take action (sign up, make an enquiry, buy the product/service, etc.). What about the bad ones; where do you think they go wrong? And finally, what lessons can you take for your writing?

4

Learn from the professionals

- KISS
- Be topical
- Emphasise your message
- Know your audience
- Appeal to readers' self-interest
- Repeat and summarise
- The benefits of structure and signposts
- Variety is the spice of life
- Add a quote
- Provoke a response

“After nourishment, shelter and companionship, stories are the thing we need most in the world.”

Philip Pullman

In my training courses on 'How to write effectively' I show delegates some of the techniques used by/in the arena of professional writers, which I label 'the 3Ms':

◆ Mass Markets (tabloid journalists)

◆ Marketeers (writers of advertising copy)

◆ Maestros (newspaper/magazine feature writers).

As people who work as full-time writers, they have plenty of experience of how to write well for their readers. There is some overlap in the practices they use, but here are some of their best techniques (three from each of them) that should help you in your writing.

KISS

Take a look at any of our tabloid newspapers, which together attract millions of loyal readers every day, and you should notice several things about their writing style: short sentences and paragraphs; easy/familiar language; and a message that is brief and to the point.

Seeing such writing in black and white, and realising how well it gets its message across, is a good wake-up call to any of us who are surrounded by the corporate world's more long-winded style of writing. Indeed, on my training courses I sometimes use articles from *The Sun* to demonstrate this – like this one, below.

KISS – Keep It Short and Simple

Pay tribute

REMEMBRANCE Sunday was an opportunity for us all to pay public tribute to those soldiers who have died in battle.

Today is Armistice Day – a chance for private homage.

It was at the eleventh hour of the eleventh day of the eleventh month that World War 1 ended exactly 90 years ago.

> But our story of Capt David Hicks, who refused morphine despite mortal wounds, shows the heroism of our armed forces is timeless.
>
> Spare two minutes of YOUR time today to remember them.
>
> SOURCE: *The Sun*, 11 November 2008

If you want a more learned source than *The Sun*, visit the website for The Plain English Campaign, who advise that clear writing should have an average sentence length of 15–20 words. Increased length doesn't make for better sentences, nor does it make for better documents. For example, The 10 Commandments comprise just 130 words, and the US Declaration of Independence is 485, etc.

What's the link here? Well, an early lesson to any trainee journalist, reflected in the above and a motto that should help you, is KISS – 'Keep It Short and Simple' (slightly different to the same abbreviation, 'Keep it Simple, Stupid').

Be topical

What you are writing might feel important. You might also think it answers many people's needs. You might even think it *well written*. But it isn't easy to attract your target readers' attention. After all, they may be busy doing other things, are bombarded with advertising and other messages all day long, and they can go to many other places for the same product/service as yours.

Given the above, one technique commonly used by mass markets is to use headlines and sub-headings that 'hook' onto ideas *already in the news* (they also use the term 'piggyback' or 'link'). They know it is a lot easier to grab readers' attention by linking to something that might already be in their mind, or resonate, than trying to introduce something new. For example, have a look on the web how often the phrase 'Size Matters' is used as part of headlines/sub-headings, or the phrase 'Keep Calm and …'.

Key Point: Whether you are writing a new brochure, blog, web text, or whatever, try and make your writing *topical* – draw on issues, news stories, ideas, people, sayings, etc. that are likely to be already on your readers' minds. It'll help you grab their attention.

Use a 'hook' to gain attention

One of the best examples I have seen of this was a few years ago, by Crisis at Christmas.

The charity distributed a red fundraising flyer (i.e. using Christmas colours to catch people's attention) that was shaped, and looked like, a tall menu card – but it had a difference. Each of the different courses described aspects of support that Crisis offered anyone who was homeless, and to which readers were being asked to donate.

So, the Starters were: A hot meal and Companionship (for people who were homeless). The Main Courses were: A health check, Specialist services, Specialist advice and Housing. The Desserts were: New skills and New hope. Each of them had a short, one or two sentence description beneath.

Buying a 'meal' (i.e. reminiscent of going to a restaurant over Christmas with friends, but in practice making a donation to Crisis of £23.39), would pay for a homeless person to receive all these elements of support over the Christmas period.

Emphasise your message

I mentioned above how I sometimes use articles from *The Sun* in my training courses. Well, one of their editorials now in front of me – about relations between the police and journalists – uses around ten different types of formatting to emphasise its message. They are: larger font size, bold, underline, italics, capitals…plus combinations of these of course… and more subtly, words within dashes, and question marks.

I don't advise using *too many* methods of emphasis on any one page, which can result in your text becoming aesthetically unattractive and detract from your content – and *The Sun* can go over the limit at times, as here. However, corporate copywriting can be rather conservative, and there is no harm in using some of these methods to emphasise your message and make it clear to the reader.

Know your audience

People who spend millions on advertising need to *really know* their audience if their advertisements are going to work. They have to know the people they are targeting, and what makes them tick. Newspapers and in particular specialist magazines have to do the same; they draw up readership profiles to remind their writers who they are writing for and also to help secure advertising. (See Chapter 3.)

Do *you* know your audience? Having an imaginary profile of them in your head will help you shape your writing: what sort of language to use, what content and issues to address, and what things they are influenced by.

It might take a bit of market research, or teasing out readers' details, but knowing your audience will help shape your writing, pose the right questions, think like them, and get your message across.

Appeal to readers' self-interest

Marketeers know what makes us tick. They know what we are influenced by. They know that, by tapping into our emotions, they can nudge us into reading their text, contacting them, and ultimately buying their product/service.

Look at some of the advertising copy around you – the ones that catch your attention and are persuasive. The chances are that they highlight how their product is: bigger/better/faster, will sort out your worries, remove/address your fears, make you more liked/loved, enable you to live some of the life you dream of, etc. Add some of that to your writing! Here are some examples that were pushed through my door only recently.

Know what will persuade your readers

◆ Take the first step towards a better life in 2015. [David Lloyd Leisure]

◆ Ultimate garden recliner and cantilever parasol. Relax in the summer sun in complete comfort…[Garden recliner and parasol, from *The Independent*]

◆ Insurance and support. To avoid mobile misery. [Geek Squad, Carphone Warehouse]

◆ Adventures in Excellence. [M&S]

◆ Make the week-end last a lifetime. [Swansea Bay]

COMMENTS: Promises work wonders in persuading people ('a better life in 2015', 'relax in complete comfort', 'make the week-end last a lifetime'), as does removing their worries ('avoid mobile misery').

Repeat and summarise

Many advertisements repeat and summarise their key points – once, if not twice. People being interviewed by the media do the same – politicians, in particular. All of them know that their readers/listeners/viewers may not have seen/heard their key point the first time round. Also, repeating something is another way of showing how important it is, and that the audience should take note.

In contrast, the convention in most writing is to *avoid repetition* – to show the range of our vocabulary and give the readers variety. But is that right in this instance? The chances are that, for much of your writing, your readers were not paying 100 per cent attention.

My view is, repeat and summarise; it helps get your message across. As the old army adage for giving speeches goes: 'Tell them what you are going to tell them. Tell them. Then tell them what you told them.'

The benefits of structure and signposts

Feature articles in newspapers and magazines can be 500+ words, and as a result they need to be well structured. But they don't want to use the rigid format of news stories (which go from the newest and most important details to the least), and they don't have the advantages of magazines and brochures (which can use page layout to direct readers around their content). So, how do they do it?

Here are three techniques used by feature writers, which you might find helpful:

- **'Nub' paragraph** – This tells the reader what the feature is about, and why they should read it.

- **Signposts (major)** – Phrases used to inform the reader about the text that follows, or to summarise what has just been covered. They often occur at the start of a paragraph. For example: *'There are three reasons for this ...'*, *'In this section we cover ...'*, *'Here's what our customers say ...'*.

- **Signposts (minor)/Link words** – Same as the above, but single words/shorter phrases, and can occur at the start or midway through a paragraph. For example: *'First, ...'*, *'For this reason, ...'*, *'However, ...'*, *'In summary, ... '*, etc.

I say more about the importance of structuring your work, and the gains to be had from it, in Chapters 10–13

Variety is the spice of life

It might sound strange but getting readers' attention depends not just on *what* you write, and *how well* you write, it is also influenced by what your writing *sounds like* – the sounds of words, the rhythm created by the words and punctuation in each sentence, and the variation in your sentences' length.

To help make your writing engage better with readers, write sentences of different length, avoid using too many conjunctions (*and, but, also*, etc.) in successive sentences, and put in the occasionally really short sentence, whose meaning will really stand out as a result. All of these will make your document an easier read – enjoyable, even.

> **Key Point:** A good way to test your writing and to spot if any sections need editing is to read your work out loud. You will quickly spot any sections where, for example, the narrative is slow rather than lively, the rhythm is monotonous rather than varied, and if any sentences are too long.

Add a quote

When a journalist returns to his/her office after working on a story, the first thing an editor will usually ask them is, 'Did you get a good quote?'

Why do editors love quotes? For several reasons. First, they can make a piece come alive – by being strong and telling, by providing a good summary of the story, or having memorable wording. Secondly, they can be used in the design/layout ('pull-out quotes', in a larger font size, can break up the text and influence people to read it). And thirdly, part of them can be used in the headline or 'standfirst', which is the one or more sentences below the headline that describe an article in more detail (common in magazines in particular).

One final reason. At the end of the day we are all humans, and we relate best to other people. So every good editor knows that no amount of description engages or tells a story better than a good quote.

Provoke a response

One common ingredient in the tips from my '3Ms', in this chapter, is that your writing will be much better if you think carefully, before you start, *what you want the reader to do* as a result of reading your text, and how you will best achieve that.

Thinking about this first, before you write – e.g. are you trying to *sell them* something, to *influence* their thinking, to *convince* them of an argument, etc. – makes sure you concentrate on what words to use, the most persuasive arguments, the key data, etc. Far better to work this into your head beforehand, than trying to weave it into your text when editing.

Further reading

The Plain English Campaign. Free guides. General guides – How to write plain English. Available at: www.plainenglish.co.uk/free-guides.html

Write it Right – John Peck and Martin Coyle. Palgrave Macmillan, 2012.

Practice writing exercises

Read the editorial of a tabloid newspaper, or a piece by one of their columnists (i.e. a piece by a named journalist, which is usually identifiable by having a photo/drawing of them alongside). Note the directness of their language, the techniques they use to emphasise their message, and how their writing style makes you feel/respond. Would any of their style be useful additions to your writing?

Draw up two or three profiles of your target customers, as per p. 13. Include information you know, and information that you don't know but would be useful. Build on these profiles and have them at hand when you write for different customers.

Take one of your bits of writing from the exercises in Chapter 2 or 3. Now add five of the ideas suggested in this chapter – e.g. a quote, varying your sentence length, use a signpost, etc. Re-read the text out loud, and see the effect of your additions. Which ones do you think worked well, and where can you apply them to your writing?

Sometimes we write in an overly formal style when writing letters and reports at work, writing in a language that we would never use when speaking. As a way to reduce this, listen to yourself when talking to a customer on the phone, or when dealing with someone face to face. Now inject the same 'softer language' you used on those occasions into some of your business writing (you can include anecdotes, light-hearted jokes, etc.).

5

Who's talking?

" We often refuse to accept an idea merely because the tone of voice in which it has been expressed is unsympathetic to us. **"**

Friedrich Nietzsche

It is important that your writing has the right 'tone of voice' (i.e. what your writing sounds like as a result of the words you use, writing style, etc.), which affects your ability to connect or not with your target audience. Showing that you are tuned into your audience's way of thinking, way of speaking, needs and constraints, etc., shows you are on their wavelength. This will help you engage better, and help you sell your products and services.

If you are in any doubt about the meaning and importance of your tone of voice, think how you adjust your spoken language according to whether you are talking to your partner, friend, someone from your family, a work colleague … person in the street, shop assistant, bus/train conductor, complete stranger, person in authority, etc. Alternatively, think how your tone of voice changes according to whether you are writing a thank you letter, letter of complaint, a request to get on a tender list, or a rallying call to your staff.

Getting the right tone of voice really matters.

Writing with a voice

At the age of 30 I was a penniless beach bum. At the age of 37, I was a millionaire. I honestly believe that anyone – absolutely anyone – can do exactly what I did and turn their life around; you just have to wake up to the possibilities that are all around you and make a decision to change your life.

I left school at 15 without any qualifications. At 19, I was dishonourably discharged from the Royal Navy. For the next ten years I made ends meet with a series of dead-end-jobs – cabbying, selling ice-creams on the beach, bar work, fixing up old motors – until I found myself sitting on a beach one day wondering where I was headed.

COMMENTS: Duncan Bannatyne reveals his character through a strong voice at the start of his self-help book. His voice and language make us feel he is someone who does not mince his words (e.g. 'penniless beach bum', 'fixing up old motors') and is a high-achiever who does not hang around, so must be worth listening to (in just seven years, or 20 words, he turned his life around and became a millionaire). He uses good punctuation to stress his key points ('anyone – absolutely anyone'), and his uplifting language; with the main message emphasised by placing it at the end of the sentence, are just the inspirational talk his readers want ('wake up to the possibilities ... make a decision to change your life').

SOURCE: *Wake Up and Change Your Life* – Duncan Bannatyne. Orion Books, 2009.

What would you be?

As a light-hearted start to finding your voice, ask yourself, if your product or service were, for example, a car, a type of animal, or breed of dog, what would it be? Your decision may help you start to characterise the product, service, or brand you want to be seen as.

Decide your values

Now let's get more serious. You should be able to describe your organisation (or a particular brand within it) in two or three values – beliefs that you have about yourself, that should be imputed into your writing. (If you come up with any more than three you risk duplication, or obsessing over less important, minor values.)

Here are some examples, for some different products:

Brand	Values
Organic yoghurt	Honest, Friendly, Principled
Children's shoes	Fun, Practical, Economical
IT support company	Reliable, Proactive, Knowledgeable.

Now, how would you describe *your* organisation's/brand's values? Try to incorporate them into your writing; they should come through to the reader.

Your writing style

A variant on the above use of *values* is to think how you want to project to others through your writing *style* (which might also affect the design of your literature, your presentation and appearance, etc.).

Here are some examples of different writing styles, in pairs that are polar opposites of one another (e.g. formal or informal). Some of the choices may not be appropriate to your particular product or service, or your kind of writing. But for those that are, think how you want your writing to sound.

Formal or Informal
Serious or Light-hearted
Friendly or Aloof
Lively or Slow
Subjective or Objective
Opinionated or Open-minded
Enthusiastic or Dull
Any others?

Want inspiration?

If you want help or inspiration in deciding your values and writing style, you will find that some businesses/organisations publish quite comprehensive documents on their branding on their websites. Here are a few I found on the web in 2015, which you might find useful.

Examples of business branding

The City of Edinburgh – describes the essence of its brand as 'a city with a drama and a magical quality … bursting with ideas and life … a city of contrasts … that stimulates senses and imagination.'

London's Kew Gardens – describes its personality as 'pioneering and confident, trusted and intelligent, friendly and welcoming, and entrepreneurial and savvy'.

The NHS – stresses to its staff that their communications need to be (among other things): 'clear and professional, cost-effective, straightforward, modern, accessible, honest and respectful'.

The British Council – describes its tone of voice as aiming to be: 'worldly, inspiring, inclusive, vivid and authoritative'.

SOURCE: From their websites

The power of vocabulary

The vocabulary you use is another ingredient of your tone of voice, and this too will affect whether or not you connect with your audience. To guide their staff, businesses with a strong brand will have a 'dictionary' of words they want them to use, and words that they specifically don't. You may want to do the same.

Don't forget to think whether you allow industry jargon, clichés and abbreviations (and symbols such as & and !). Using these can help show you are on the right wavelength (e.g. the use of fashionable or industry-specific buzzwords), but some people may be less familiar with these terms, and may even be put off by them.

Using vocabulary to engage readers

IT'S JUST A SHOWER ISN'T IT? You could say that. Or you could say it's a Samuel Heath 'Fairfield' shower. You could point out that it's been meticulously formed from the purest European brass; then hand-polished and chrome-plated in up to 34 individual processes. You could say it's manufactured entirely in the UK and it's passed over 500 hours of salt spray and humidity testing. You could say it'll last a lifetime. Or, of course, you could insist that it's just a shower…

COMMENTS: Who would have thought of advertising a *shower* like this, but why not? The language in this advertisement really jumped out at me, and should catch the eye of anyone who loves showers. The descriptive prose ('hand-polished', 'meticulously formed') conjures up a lovely image, and an exclusive product. The detailed specifications ('chrome-plated in up to 34 individual processes') convey a uniqueness – and will fascinate gadget lovers. A lovely rhythm is created by mixing short and long sentences (from 4–24 words in length), and the use of repetition ('You could say…'). To cap it all, the shower will fulfil customers' dreams ('it'll last a lifetime').

SOURCE: Start of Samuel Heath shower advertisement, *The Independent*

… and dialogue

Using dialogue is another feature that gives you a strong tone of voice, and will help you connect better with readers (I mean *actual* dialogue e.g. 'Your services are brilliant', said Helen Williams; not reported speech, like 'Helen Williams said our services were "brilliant"'). A quote or two such as this adds a bit of life or colour to a passage of text – as well as someone else's voice. Think of how testimonials can achieve the same.

Plus mood...

This also affects your tone of voice. You may be positive (e.g. 'We will steer the business through the difficult economic climate and come out much stronger after it.') or you may want to be more circumspect (e.g. 'We will seek to avoid the worst of the recession, so that the business can survive.'). In general, a more positive tone will be appropriate, but there may be occasions where you don't want to sound overconfident. Which is appropriate for your text?

... and grammar

Your tone will also influenced by your decisions on the following, more grammatical issues.

Sentence length

Overly long sentences will give your writing a more learned and academic style, as well as running the risk (especially if they have poor punctuation) of being confusing to the reader. Do you want to set a maximum sentence length in your text?

In contrast, there is no harm in short sentences. Like this. Varying the length of your sentences creates a good rhythm, as in this paragraph.

Punctuation

Be careful of using too many colons, semi-colons and dashes (–), which increase sentence length and can therefore create a heavy, rather than snappy, writing style.

Pronouns

If you use the first person pronoun (I/me) and the second (you) your writing will sound more friendly and inclusive to the reader. This compares with using the third person (he, she, it), or just referring to your organisation by its name, which can sound a bit off-hand and distant. Using the first and second person is particularly important for website text, which otherwise can seem distant and impersonal.

Contractions (can't, haven't, we'll, etc.)?

Allowing these in your text will make your writing quite light and relaxed, like everyday speech; but if you use them too much you can sound *too informal* (and some people believe you shouldn't use them in business letters). In addition to the contractions above, there are also older abbreviations and Cockney Slang such as: 'em (them), 'er (her), 'im (him). It all depends on what effect you want.

Active or passive tense

Sentences can either be written in what is called the active voice/tense (sometimes described as 'who did what') or the passive ('what was done by whom'). The passive is identified by an auxiliary verb (part of the verb to have/to be/to get) followed by a past participle of the main verb. Using the active is generally thought preferable, as it produces shorter sentences and gives a feeling of movement (e.g. *The committee presented a report* versus *A report was presented by the committee*, where *'was presented'* is in the passive tense).

However, there are occasions where the passive should be, and is, used (as well as sometimes just for variety). To explain further, note that using the passive means *who* is doing the action is not written until the end of the sentence, if at all. So the passive tense will be used if *who is responsible* is: (i) not known and therefore need not be stated (e.g. *A man has been shot in the park*); (ii) you may not want to identify them (*Proposals for a proposed multi-million leisure have been rejected*); or (iii) if they are less important than who has been affected (*Prince Charles was shot earlier today by Joe Blogs*).

Examples of good corporate copywriting

If you want examples of how to put all the above ideas into your copywriting, take a closer look at some of the everyday brands around you. In the box are some examples of high-street brands that, I think, have a strong and attractive tone of voice – ingredients worth aspiring to in your writing.

Examples of good copywriting

Pret A Manger

Our kitchens get replenished with wonderful ingredients early each morning and our Hot Chefs are often the first through the door. In their quest to keep our shelves full of oven-fresh, homely hot food, they bake in small batches. Little and often is the key. Straight from the kitchen. Hot off the shelves.

COMMENTS: Note the accessible language (our); the images and messages ('oven-fresh, homely hot food... small batches'); and how short sentences are used to emphasise the final messages ('Little and often is the key. Straight from the kitchen. Hot off the shelves.').

Innocent Drinks

hello, we're innocent

...and we're here to make it easy for people to do themselves some good (whilst making it taste nice too). We started innocent in 1999 after selling our smoothies at a music festival. We put up a big sign asking people if they thought we should give up our jobs to make smoothies, and put a bin saying 'Yes' and a bin saying 'No' in front of the stall. Then we got people to vote with their empties. At the end of the weekend, the 'Yes' bin was full, so we resigned from our jobs the next day and got cracking.

Since then we've started making veg pots, juices and kids' drinks, in our quest to make natural, delicious, healthy foods that help people live well and die old.

COMMENTS: Note the impact of everyday and immediate language ('hello, we're innocent'); their energy ('we resigned from our jobs the next day and got cracking'); and messages placed at the end of the sentence, and said plainly and powerfully ('natural, delicious, healthy foods ... that help people live well and die old').

SOURCE: Respective websites. Other corporate copywriting also worth looking at are, for example, the websites of: Cranks, Method, Starbucks and Urban Eat.

Key Point: We spend the day communicating and being communicated to – in spoken language, written words and/or body language – and as a result we absorb the styles around us, e.g. when we read particular authors, hear new words/phrases, etc. So, if you read authors/newspapers whose writing style you like, or want to emulate, you will adopt some of their practices. Remember, the best tone of voice is a simple, grown-up language. Avoid dull, monotonous, ubiquitous, meaningless corporate speak.

Further reading

Brand Success – Matt Haig. Kogan Page, 2011.

Copywriting: successful writing for design, advertising and marketing – Mark Shaw. Laurence King, 2009.

Creative Writing – Adele Ramèt. How To Books, 2008.

Practice writing exercises

How you would describe *your* organisation's/brand's values and writing style, as per p. 45?

Make a list of the vocabulary you like to use, and try to *avoid using*, when describing your products/services to customers – as per p. 47. To check your thinking is right, test the two lists with suitable members of your family and/or friends, i.e. those who could be customers.

Take a mass mailing letter (e.g. a free brochure, charity appeal, letter from an MP/councillor) that you think has the wrong tone of voice for engaging with you. Rewrite it in a tone that connects better with you. If necessary, you can change the structure and the amount of information. Now, have you got your tone of voice right in *your writing*?

Take a look at the writing styles of some of the following high-street brands, either on their websites, in their shops or products: Pret A Manger, Starbucks, Innocent Drinks, Method, Cranks, Urban Eat (and any others you think are good). Are there aspects of their writing that you like, and why; and can you incorporate them into *your* writing?

6

Grab readers' attention

- Impactful introductions
- AIDA/AIDCA model

66 The beginning is the most important part of the work. 99

Plato

Impactful introductions

Whatever you are writing, it is essential to have a good heading and introduction – whether you are writing web text or blogs, case studies or project summaries, brochures or reports.

The start of your document has the power to hook your readers' interest, and gives the first impressions of you and your business/organisation. In contrast, your ending gives them their lasting memories, and can nudge them into doing what you want. (These principles also apply to sentences, paragraphs and longer documents).

Your introduction is also likely to be read more than once, so can shape readers' views.

Below are ten commonly used types of introduction, with examples, for you to draw on and get inspiration. But these are just ten; if you look around you'll find plenty of others.

Facts/Statistics

- *23% of men shave less than three times a week.*

- *Seven reasons why our 3D smartphone technology will change the market forever.*

Questions

- *Did you know that Wembley Stadium has more toilets than any other building in the world?* (2,618 apparently).

- *Want to overhaul your marketing? Looking for a wow factor? Something to blow your competition away?* [Start of a brochure written by me for Hunts, a print, marketing and design agency in Oxford.]

Significant quote

- *'Officially there are no deer in Wales', says Jackie Symmons.*

Scene-setter

- *William, 10, has just added smashing his neighbour's greenhouse to his list of crimes.*

◆ *BURSTING WITH CHOICE* [Argos catalogue.]

Anecdote/Story

◆ *It used to be easy for self-builders. They would find plots, often at bargain prices, then win consent from planners...*

Description/Atmosphere

◆ *A MOTHER'S DREAM. Learn how families in Nepal are changing the future – and how you can help them realise their dreams.* [Oxfam fundraising leaflet.]

◆ *Eternal optimist: Some people never wake up on the wrong side of the bed. Life through coloured glasses. Must be nice. Soothing + always skin friendly. Naturally delivered.* [Label on body wash produced by Method Home Products.]

Dramatic/Intriguing

◆ *Turn your words into money: how to write effective fundraising copy and direct mail.* [Workshop description, Directory of Social Change.]

Cryptic/Play on words

◆ *Mum's the WORD* [Headline to article from business magazine about a woman stopping commuting and going self-employed so that she could spend more time with her children.]

◆ *Too Posh to Wash* [Title of a report by 2020 Health into standards of nursing in the NHS: An investigation of why lapses occur and how they can be reduced.]

◆ *Bosom Friends* [Title of leaflet produced by Oxfordshire Breast Cancer Support Group.]

Celebrity hook

◆ *Buddha – now there was a nice chap. Never said a bad word about anyone, and always kept his stereo at a respectable volume so as not to disturb the neighbours...* [Smoothie, from Innocent Drinks.]

Summarising

- *A great feature is a girl's best friend. It offers advice, belly laughs, a gripping story and a water-cooler of hard facts.* [Start of a magazine feature article.]

AIDA/AIDCA model

Another way to grab your readers is to draw on a very well-used model for how to structure any kind of copywriting, from introduction through to ending, called AIDA.

AIDA stands for grabbing readers' **Attention**, then stimulating their **Interest** and convincing them of their **Desire**, and concludes with giving them a clear Call to **Action** (i.e. what you want them to *do*). Although this is the normal sequence, note that some steps can overlap (e.g. Desire and Interest) and some are not restricted to that position (e.g. your Call to Action may come *several times* in your document, not just at its end.)

The model is commonly said to have been first used by US advertisers of soap products in the 1950s, although there is evidence something similar was also used by the Greek philosopher Aristotle and others, as a guide to successful oration.

I like the slightly amended version, AIDCA, where the additional C stands for giving readers **Conviction**. Either way, let me explain the letters in more detail. After them, I also give an example of a flyer I wrote that follows this model.

A = Grab your audience's **Attention** in your headline/introduction

The importance of grabbing your reader should now be familiar to you. But not, it seems, to everyone. For example, I am constantly amazed how many email newsletters I get with a dull subject line, like 'Latest newsletter from …', and yet that is the first and only thing I see when they arrive in my email inbox. Could that be any *less* interesting? From my experience, we are all inundated with emails, and a subject line like that example gives us the perfect reason *to delete it.*

In contrast, the ten ideas above are a lot more eye-catching. Within them, I think questions can be particularly effective at engaging your readers, e.g. *'Looking for ways to save on recruitment costs?'*, and headlines that suggest you can answer their wants or needs, like *'How mind mapping can double your sales.'*

On a final note, don't let your headlines be too long, which I often have to point out when helping organisations with their websites. A headline needs to jump out at the reader. It shouldn't have to be 'read' word for word (*Don't Make Me Think* is the title of a famous book on how to write for the web, by Seth Godin) and should definitely not span more than one line. I would suggest around 10–14 words as the limit.

I = Stimulate their **Interest** by putting yourself in their shoes

Once you have got your readers hooked you need to get them more *interested* e.g. by describing your product/service and how it might help them. Make sure you relate to their situation and get to your point quick, e.g. *'Learn how to drive traffic to your website.'* Or put a few of your key messages in bullet points, so they are clear to your readers and they are interested to read further.

D = Convince them of their **Desire** by outlining your offer, etc.

As early as possible make people *desire* what you are offering, which is usually done by highlighting the benefits of your product/service. We often focus on our products' features (e.g. central locking of car doors), and their advantages (you don't need to go to each door), but it is the benefits (peace of mind) that are going to sway customers. Other examples of strong benefits would be: you will save people time or money; make them healthier, happier or safer; etc.

To increase readers' desire you could also offer them a free trial, or a discounted price.

Some people use the 'So what?' test here. This involves identifying the benefit(s) you are offering readers and checking, as far as you can tell, that a typical reader won't just say 'So what?' i.e. your benefits *are* meaningful and relevant to them.

C = Give them **Conviction**, using testimonials etc.

Now that you have got potential customers' interest and desire, you need to **convince** them that *yours* (rather than anyone else's) is the right product/ service. Typically this is done by citing other people's views: e.g. using testimonials, back-up research, press coverage, or anything convincing.

Ideally, your offer is something that seems really valuable to them but actually costs you nothing. Like, *'Orders shipped in 48 hours'* (if you always achieve that anyway) or *'Money-back guarantee'* (if the law entitles them to that anyway), etc.

A = Present a clear 'Call to **Action**'

And finally, think *what you want people to do* as a result of reading your document, and make sure you spell it out clearly. Don't make people drift off to another supplier, or have to search for how to contact you. For example, do you want people to visit your website, leave their email address – which?

And remember, don't just put your Call to Action at the end of the document; it will be easier for people to find, and should have more influence, if it is in several places.

On the next page is an abbreviated example of a Facebook advertisement that I prepared for a client, using the AIDCA model.

Flyer using AIDCA Model

Carol lost 5 stone in 1 year – <u>WITHOUT</u> going to a gym YOU can too!

Interested?

Discover what she did … and how it can work for you

Carol's story...

"I used to weigh over 18 stone. Then one day I made a decision to lose weight. And inside one year I lost … an amazing 5 stone. No Gym! No Gastric Band! No Surgery!"

◆ Are you overweight?

◆ Got chronic diseases in your family?

◆ Want to know more?

Come and hear Carol's story – in London <u>this week</u>

You will learn exactly how she got from 18 stone down to 13.

You will discover...

◆ How to be LIGHTER without going to the gym.

◆ How to be FITTER without going to the gym.

◆ How to be HEALTHIER without going to the gym.

Please register to ensure yourself a place (first come first served).

Benefits from attending

◆ Learn Carol's secrets for losing SEVERAL stone.

◆ Go home with lessons, tips, ideas … and more.

◆ Be inspired that YOU CAN ACHIEVE THE SAME.

Post Script ...

Carol has benefitted some more. Thanks to losing weight, and other changes, she has significantly reduced her risk to chronic diseases – including Cancer, Alzheimer's and Heart Disease.

A prize worth having?

To hear Carol's story, book your place <u>TODAY</u>.

"It changed my life," she says, "and it can change yours, too."

Further reading

Writing for journalists – Wynford Hicks. Routledge, 2008.

Practice writing exercises

To hook your readers, you must have a good opening to your case studies, blogs, brochures, etc. Be bold, and don't waffle with a long preamble. One source of ideas is to look how professionals like novelists do it. So, here are some famous first lines from books, followed by an explanation of their effectiveness and an example by me of how they can be copied. Once you have examined them, make up *your own* examples. If you want to try *other* first lines of books, it is easy to find more on the web.

◆ 'It was a bright cold day in April and the clocks were striking thirteen.' (A clock striking thirteen, in George Orwell's *1984*, is very dramatic, and immediately it tells readers this is a very different world.) – What about, 'I was sitting at my office desk, ready for work, when a client jumped out of my coffee.'

◆ 'The past is a foreign country. They do things differently there.' (They are only two short sentences, but they create intrigue and anticipation to the start of L.P. Hartley's *The Go-Between*.) – What about, 'Social Media is a world unto itself. It operates under different rules.'

◆ 'It is a truth universally acknowledged, that a single man in possession of a good fortune, must be in want of a wife.' (Suspense until the last word of the sentence in Jane Austen's *Pride and Prejudice*) – What about, 'It is a fundamental principle that the most important aspect of promoting ones products, and it applies to whatever kind of marketing you adopt, is to assess the effectiveness of your results – to measure.'

Over the course of a few days or weeks (depending on how many emails you get), make a note of the e-newsletters and general emails (i.e. *not* those from customers and people known to you) that you open and read. How much impact do their *subject lines* have on your decisions, and which are the most and least effective at persuading you to open the emails? Are there any lessons for you, in the headings to *your* emails, e-newsletters, etc.?

Write several different starts to one of your recent writings (e-newsletter, flyer, advert or email subject line, etc.), using the types of introduction listed at the start of this chapter (or others). Decide which ones you like best, and why.

Plan a short, one-page flyer for one of your products/services, using the AIDCA model outlined in this chapter. At the side of your text, note what stage of AIDCA each sentence/paragraph refers to. Test the effectiveness of your work on someone else, or by re-reading it a few weeks later.

7

How to overcome writing's challenges

- Make *starting* writing as easy as possible
- Don't know how to start/Fear 'the blank page'
- Maximise the time you write
- Dealing with writer's block
- Short of inspiration?
- Overloaded with content
- Lost confidence in your writing?
- Struggling to keep going
- Facing a deadline
- Can't find time to write

66 If you get stuck, get away from your desk. Take a walk, take a bath, go to sleep, make a pie, draw, listen to music, meditate, exercise; whatever you do, don't just sit there scowling at the problem. Open a gap for your words, create a space. Be patient. 99

Hilary Mantel

Writing isn't easy. Even the more experienced of us can sometimes get stuck, have 'off days', and fail to make the progress we wanted. This chapter provides ideas for sorting out the commonly encountered challenges.

Make *starting* writing as easy as possible

Start collating relevant material *before* you start writing. This will reduce the pressure of the 'Big Day', the blank page, and give you some solid material and a place to start writing.

Also, start your writing at a section you are most confident or knowledgeable about – NOT at the beginning, which can be the hardest to write and is often best written last.

Don't know how to start/Fear 'the blank page'

Do you have a plan for your overall content, and is it detailed enough for you to know what you are writing?

Do you have clear objectives for whatever you are writing, and do you have a clear idea of *who* you are writing for? Spell them out – it will give you confidence about what you are writing.

> **Key Point:** One technique many people find useful for guiding their writing is to make a mind map of the overall content, and if necessary for each section. This will help you get a vision of where different things go, how they fit together, and provide you with a clear plan for each time you write.

Maximise the time you write

Choose the time, place and environment which suits you best to write. It may be 5am in the kitchen, with no other sounds and when nobody else is awake. Or it may be 10pm in your office, with your preferred music or radio station blaring away in the background. Whenever and whatever works best *for you*.

Clear your desk of distractions – so that you can focus on your writing.

Clear your mind of anything that may interfere with your writing – e.g. make a list of the jobs, phone calls, etc. that you need to get done today, or if necessary get them done before you start.

Get some exercise; better still, get some two or three times each week.

Dealing with writer's block

Would a change of scene help, i.e. *where* you write? I find I sometimes get bored of working in my office; however, I can get a burst of creativity (that then carries me through several days or weeks) if I work somewhere different for a while – a library, coffee shop, friend's house, etc.

Remind yourself *why* you are writing, and what your writing is going to achieve. Summarise it on a note, and position it on the wall in front of you – so that you see it and are stimulated by it. Visualising the outcome and what it is going to do for you should provide some energy to get you going.

Some people may find it helpful to take a break from writing for a few days – or *weeks* if necessary, and they have time. Letting your writing job submerge from the top of your mind will mean that when you come back to it you will be clear-thinking and refreshed.

Others may not be comfortable about taking a break and might instead benefit from the disciple of *writing something every day*. Why? First, *something* is better than nothing, and it can always be edited later. Secondly, the process of writing will release some creativity in you, which should remove your block.

Short of inspiration?

Get ideas and inspiration from others. Depending on what you are writing, look for ideas from the web, business magazines, in libraries and bookshops, wherever. See what examples and writing styles grab you; try and identify why; and then copy their techniques.

> **Key Point:** Make a mental note of articles, books, etc. whose writing style you like. Read more of them and you will assimilate some of their good practice.

Overloaded with content

Step away from your writing, for example by going for a walk, doing some shopping, or doing a small job. This should help you stand back from your text, and give you an overview of all your material and how things will best fit together.

If you have written too much, print it out, get a 'red pen', and delete anything not absolutely crucial to your subject, message or objectives. Better still, work out your word length *before you start writing* (and the length for each section), which will force you to decide, as you write, what there is space for and what there isn't.

Lost confidence in your writing?

This can affect all of us at times. My suggestion is take a look at some other things you have written in the past, and remind yourself where they were used, and people's reaction, etc. This should remind you that you *can* write.

In fact, what is more likely than bad writing is that your work has just become overly familiar to you – it no longer seems new or original – and *that* has caused your doubt. Your writing is probably fine.

One final idea: each time you sit down to write, make sure you have a clear plan of what you are writing in *that session*, and that you know how it fits into your plan for the overall content.

Struggling to keep going

Break your overall job into manageable chunks; work on them bit by bit, allocating times when you will write each of them. Gradually you will get the job done.

Taking a mini-break, say for just 20–30 minutes, can really help clear your head. Even better if you can get a tedious household job done at the same time, like the washing up – which will give you a boost, won't therefore be hanging over you, and doesn't have to be done later.

Sweets are also said to improve concentration!

Announcing to others when your work is going to be finished might sound a bit severe, but for some people it does just the trick. It can ensure you keep writing, to avoid any embarrassment and feeling of 'failure'.

Facing a deadline

Write without any major editing as you go along, which has three benefits. It will boost your creativity, which will mean you write faster; it means you focus on the writing rather than the dwindling time available; and it will ensure you at least write *something* – which is far better than nothing, and can always be edited later.

However, editing at the end of each writing session can also be a good idea, to stop you from writing too much and stop you from forgetting what you were trying to say.

Try to keep going. I know it's obvious but the more you stop (even if it's to do comforting things like making a cup of tea/coffee), the less time you have … and time may be against you.

Can't find time to write

Make a commitment to your writing by blocking out a specific time for it in your diary. This should nudge you into doing it, and mean you don't commit yourself to other things, or accept invitations to things that could distract or divert you.

Try using a voice recorder or speech recognition software (e.g. Dragon), which can make writing easier and faster. However, still plan your content as if you were writing, so you know exactly what you are going to say and don't therefore have to spend ages editing it later.

> **Key Point:** Set yourself targets for the number of words to write by given dates, with rewards if you meet them – larger ones for larger achievements. Or use a writing buddy, to whom you commit yourself to sending a certain number of pages/words on a regular basis, e.g. at the end of each week.

Further reading

How to be a Writer – Stewart Ferris. Summerscale, 2013.

Perfect Text blog. Available at: www.perfecttext.org/blog/

Practice writing exercises

Think of a subject you feel comfortable writing about – like a hobby, an interest, something to do with work, whatever. Now plan a piece of writing on the topic using a mind map as p. 64.

What time of day do you work best – and where? (Try some different places if necessary.) Now try doing some of your writing then and there, rather than in your office. My guess is that you will be a lot more creative and productive.

Do 10 minutes of 'free writing' (with as little editing as possible as you write) on one of the following topics: 'Why I love…', 'Why I hate…' or 'My ideal week-end'. Notice that by the end of 10 minutes you will be getting into the subject and writing fairly fluently – which you can do for other writing tasks too, if you write in this way.

Tired of your subject, and/or of your writing task? Go to a library or bookshop and browse through some books on a subject you know nothing about. You might enjoy some of their content, but you will also get ideas for the layout, content, structure and writing style for *your* writing. Alternatively, do this on the web.

Part 3

Achieving Your Goals

8

Ways to make your writing memorable

- Put things in threes
- Importance of word order
- Get a good quote
- Tap into readers' senses and emotions
- Use similes, analogies and metaphors
- Play on words
- Make your writing *sound* good
- Make sure your document flows
- Emphatic structure
- Avoid 'turn-offs'

66 There are no dull subjects. There are only dull writers. 99

H. L. Mencken

Put things in threes

As you may have spotted already, the number three has special qualities in our culture and as a result is commonly used as a way to make an impact in writing/speech. I don't know where it started – The Three Kings must be one of the oldest examples – but here's a few well-known others:

◆ **Society** – We talk of three reasons to things, children learning their A-B-C, and estate agents talk of the importance of 'location, location, location.'

◆ **Politics** – Churchill spoke of 'Blood, sweat and tears' when becoming Prime Minister in the Second World War; Margaret Thatcher said 'No, no, no' to creeping European centralisation; and Tony Blair stressed the importance, once he was elected, of 'Education, education, education.'

◆ **Literature** – Shakespeare's King Lear says 'Tomorrow, tomorrow and tomorrow', and Hamlet says 'Words, words, words.' There are also lots of nursery rhymes and children's stories that use threes, such as the *Three Little Pigs* and *The Three Musketeers*.

It is all down to how many items we can be sure that people will remember. Three is no problem for most of us (hence instructions are regularly issued in threes), but once a list gets to four or five you start to lose, muddle and confuse people. So, when you are outlining the benefits of products/services, or summarising your strengths and expertise, etc., put them in threes. It sounds so much better.

Importance of word order

Something that can make a big difference to your writing is the position of words in sentences and paragraphs, in particular in longer documents.

The first few words of sentences and paragraphs engage your readers: they make the first impression. Whereas the final words are what readers remember: it's what they 'take home with them'. So, the first words of a sentence, for example, should have broad appeal, and be engaging; whereas the last ones are where you should make (or repeat) your most powerful points, using words that are short and strong (in meaning and sound).

Here's the start to a blog of mine that I hope demonstrates these points.

Using word order effectively

YOU heard it here first.

My book on Business Writing Skills – with nearly 200 practical tips (10 points on 17 subjects, each with its own dedicated chapter) – will be published in February 2015.

The book will give you advice on Punctuation and Grammar, Learning from the Professionals, Winning Media Interest, Making your Writing Memorable... and a whole lot more.

Why I wrote it

August is a hard month to be a freelancer — nobody is around, the weather is too tempting to do *real work*, etc. — so I decided that, from now on, I will dedicate every August to completing a project of my own, and in 2014 it would be writing a book.

All went well for the first two weeks. Seated at my desk, I churned out a chapter each day. But then I was offered a job that was too tempting to turn down ... so I had to return to my manuscript in September/October, to get the job done.

Below is the book's list of contents – for a discounted, advance copy, email me now.

COMMENTS: I try and catch readers' attention with an engaging start to sentences ('YOU heard it here first', 'August is a hard month', etc.) and with sub-headings ('Why I wrote it'). And to emphasise my main points I position them at the end of sentences ('published in February 2015', 'writing a book', 'whole lot more').

SOURCE: The start to one of my blogs, www.perfecttext.org/blog

---

Get a good quote

I have said it before and I will say it again, whether you are working on a brochure, new marketing material or website text/blog, 'Be sure to get a good quote.'

You might have to persuade the person you want to quote to agree to you using it; and you might have to probe hard, and to ask them several times before they come up with a quote that's something significant or telling. But a powerful and attributable quote – especially from someone other customers can relate to – will be worth the effort of collecting it. And so much better than those ones that say *'Mr XX of Canterbury...'* or *'Mrs C of Aberdeen'*, etc.

Tap into readers' senses and emotions

Another way of really engaging your reader, and getting them to remember your writing, is to tap into one of the five senses: sight, touch, smell, hearing and taste. Through these you get into readers' feelings and emotions, which is what makes most of us buy something, rather than its abstract features.

So, if you describe a scene the reader can relate to and are likely to have warm associations of, or can refer to the smells and sounds of something you refer to, your reader will enjoy the experience, and read on, wanting more. As an example, this start to a piece that I wrote for a national newspaper presents, I think, several strong visual images to the reader.

Writing with visual images

Three groups of visitors are wondering around Birmingham's Blakesley Hall, a timber-framed building more than 400 years old. There's one school group in red jerseys, and another in blue, and a mixed group of 12 women – Pakistani, Indian, Bangladeshi, Arabic and Afro-Caribbean – and their young children.

COMMENTS: This was a very striking scene. To portray the richness of the occasion to the reader I started my feature with several images

---

('timber-framed building', 'mixed group of 12 women'), colours ('one school group in red jerseys, and another in blue') and nationalities.

SOURCE: All Around The Houses – *Guardian*, 5 June 2007

Use similes, analogies and metaphors

If you want to describe or explain something to your readers that they may not be familiar with, try using a simile, analogy or metaphor. These can wake up your audience, help them understand what you are talking about, and provide another angle to your story.

All three involve comparing things, but analogies and metaphors (which are a type of analogy) both involve 'figurative language' – taking something *familiar* to the reader to evoke, describe or explain something that is *unfamiliar*.

Simile

These are easy to spot as they usually feature the words 'like' or 'as'. For example:

◆ *He is as hungry as a horse*

◆ *The news spread like wildfire*

◆ *Venice is like eating an entire box of chocolates in one go*

◆ *Humour can be dissected, as a frog can, but the thing dies in the process*

◆ *I slept like a log (overused ones like this are called clichés).*

Analogy

These can make unfamiliar concepts more understandable to the reader. However, be careful of analogies; they sometimes appear good at first glance/on the surface, but, if dissected, can seem less powerful and undermine your statement. (Unlike similes and metaphors, analogies can comprise several sentences.)

- *Life is a box of chocolates.*

- *I am going to be toast when I get home.*

- *Just as a sword is the weapon of a warrior, a pen is the weapon of a writer.*

- *Just as a caterpillar comes out of its cocoon, so we must come out of our comfort zone.*

- *The structure of an atom is like a solar system. The nucleus is the sun and electrons are the planets revolving around their sun.*

Metaphor

A type of analogy where a word or phrase normally used to designate one thing is used to designate another, e.g. *He* stabbed *her in the back*. Here the comparison is more indirect/implied than in similes and analogies, i.e. the wording does not literally apply (*'stabbed'*).

- *The rat race*

- *She has a bubbly personality*

- *He has other irons in the fire*

- *The need for change bulldozed a road down the centre of my mind.*

But be careful of what are called mixed metaphors. These are when two metaphors are jumbled together, which usually happen when people are stressed, e.g. public speaking. For example, in a radio interview I once said 'people should put their head above the pulpit'. What I meant to end my sentence with, and what the metaphor is, was 'parapet'. And just to rub in my mistake the interviewer corrected me!

Here are some others from people's quoted sayings – which convey some wonderful images:

- *We want someone who can hit the ground running and sail into their first contract.*

- *They've put all their eggs in one basket and it's misfired.*

- *Labour are fighting like rats in a barrel.*

- *I'm kick-starting a drive to get employee ownership into the bloodstream.*

- *Milking the temp workers for all they were worth, the manager barked orders at them.*

- *Unless we tighten our belts, we'll sink like a stone.*

- *I don't want to say they lost sight of the big picture, but they have marched to a different drummer.*

Play on words

Humour can also make writing highly memorable – but be careful. Humour is very personal, and jokes can quickly become dated and spoil your message. However, you can also raise a smile from readers if you are good at playing with words – as long as you don't do it too frequently, and aren't too predictable/obvious.

I read a piece once about the declining number of post offices, and how placing them in churches might be a way to ensure their survival in rural communities – the latter have willing volunteers, customers and space. It was only a very short piece, but it was made very evocative – and humorous – by using words and phrases with double meanings, such as 'service', and how the solution might be 'a marriage made in heaven', and 'the answer to people's prayers'. The piece put a smile on my face, and has done the same for many many delegates on my training courses. If you can do that, you can feel proud of your writing, and will be remembered.

Make your writing *sound* good

You can also make your writing memorable, and keep your reader reading and maybe even *enjoying* your text, by paying attention to the rhythm of your sentences, and the sounds of strings of words.

If a group of your sentences are of roughly the same length they will have a very regular rhythm and will sound monotonous. More appealing therefore is writing sentences *of different length*. The same applies to music. What most people like has a mix of fast and slow sections, with a variety of stresses, etc.

One way to check your rhythm is to read your work out loud, listening for: lack of progress in the story/content, neighbouring sentences of the same length (short or long), and lack of a clear emphasis in the words. If your ear detects a weakness, think about what it lacks or has too much of. Here are several ideas that should help.

Short sentences

It's good to include an occasional short sentence, which can be good for: emphasis (it draws attention to that sentence), clarity (it expresses things boldly, in black and white) and variety (provides contrast with longer sentences).

Punctuation

Good punctuation can also help emphasise things. For example, question marks in the middle of a sentence; exclamation marks; and using dashes and colons to announce what follows. Colons can be especially powerful when only one word follows them. For example:

- *There is only one thing necessary: everything.*

- *In War: Resolution. In Defeat: Defiance. In Victory: Magnanimity. In Peace: Good Will.* [Churchill]

- *Space: the final frontier.* [Star Trek]

- *To be or not to be; that is the question.* [Shakespeare].

Alliteration

Putting words together that start with the same letter or sound – what is called alliteration – sounds good, creates a sense of pleasure for the reader and will help your text/message be remembered. Don't overdo them, however. To give you a flavour of what I mean, here are a few – historic ones, and from today's language:

- *She sells sea shells by the seashore*

- *Dead as a doornail*

- *Two for tea and tea for two*

- *Ban the bomb – Power to the people* [Anti-nuclear protests in the 1950s]

- *Your flexible friend* [Access credit card]

- *Full fathom five thy father lies...* [Shakespeare's *The Tempest*]

- *Whereat, with blade, with bloody blameful blade,/He bravely broached his boiling bloody breast ...* [This was Shakespeare making fun of the overuse of alliteration by poets of his time.]

Words with sounds

Using a word with several syllables can sound better than a short word. Also, repeating a word can give a sentence a certain rhythm (and add emphasis), e.g. *This is an offer you really really cannot ignore.*

And what about using onomatopoeia. This is a word that *sounds* like what it means, which may be a noise (e.g. *pop*), a collision (*clash*), the movement of air (*swish*), an animal sound (*buzz*), etc. They can be very powerful, especially if you make one up that it is appropriate to its meaning.

Something that also sounds good is similar sounding *vowels* next to one another (e.g. *The line of time*), or different vowels and the same consonant (*He showed his mastery and mystery of the subject*), both of which are termed assonance.

Make sure your document flows

For longer documents in particular, it is really important that your text 'flows' – so that you retain your readers' interest and attention. The analogy to rivers (as in 'flows') is a good one, and can be extended.

Your document should be like a straight-running river – rather than a stream that meanders here and there, loses its direction, and has eddies and backwaters that go nowhere. Your sentences mustn't be too long, and mustn't have unnecessary phrases and waffle that would allow the development of the core meaning to flag. And each of your paragraphs should move the subject or story on, a bit like a page-turning novel.

Emphatic structure

A repeated structure or phrase (in the same or neighbouring sentences) also creates a nice-sounding rhythm, which is pleasant to read. The repeated part may be at the start or end of the sentence, or at the start of a phrase. Here are some examples: 'He came, He saw, He conquered'; and Churchill's 'We shall fight on the beaches, we shall fight on the landing grounds, we shall fight in the fields and in the streets, we shall fight in the hills; we shall never surrender.'

Avoid 'turn-offs'

There is nothing that annoys readers more than documents written in language they are unfamiliar with, can't relate to and, worse still, don't understand. Such writing just doesn't seem to talk to or be meant for them. So the readers switch off – or they find it cringe-making and turn off.

Be careful therefore of using abbreviations and acronyms readers don't know: phrases that are now so overused they are no longer original (i.e. clichés, like *win–win situation*, *thinking outside the box*, *seamless integration*, etc.); the latest buzz words (jargon, such as *it's a no-brainer*, *touch base*, *going forward*, etc. – which may be overused and/or unclear); and just plain waffle (*What we need to do is teach horizontal organisations to expand their talent management from a narrow and tactical focus to a broad, more strategic and highly integrated systems perspective …*).

> **Key Point:** Check your writing with someone who has no connection with your business/industry, nor reasons to know what you are talking about – and see if they can understand what you are saying.

Further reading

Brilliant Business Writing – Neil Taylor. Pearson, 2011.

Correct English – Brian Pythian. Teach Yourself, 2010.

Improve Your Written English – Marion Field. How to Books, 2009.

Writing With Style – Heather Pyrcz. OUP, 2010.

Practice writing exercises

Glance through a newspaper or magazine, reading the quotes from different articles. Which quotes do you think work well and why – is it their length, the rhythm or the sound of the words, etc.? Quotes can provide good endings to articles, so take particular note of any of these.

Write, or say out loud, a short description of your day – or a memorable event that you attended recently (200–300 words). In your description, use one simile in each sentence; then redo it with an analogy in each sentence; and then with metaphors.

Take one of your bits of writing from the exercises in Chapter 2 or 3, or a brochure for one of your products/services. Now edit the text to give it an attractive rhythm and make it sound good, using the ideas of short sentences, punctuation, alliteration, etc. in this chapter.

Take a paragraph of your writing, ideally one that you haven't worked on much or are not too happy with. Explore how changing the first and final few words, as described on pp. 74–5, can really change the text's impact.

Describe a customer or colleague using ten different metaphors. For example, if this person were a car, what car would they be? Now write a few for yourself!

9

Persuading your readers

66 People make emotional buying decisions, then use logic to justify them. 99

Anon

Writing persuasive text that wins over the hearts and minds of customers is an art in itself, drawing as much on psychology as writing skills. But help from such writers doesn't come cheap, so I hope this chapter can get you started.

Define your objectives

Before you start writing, spend a moment thinking carefully about what your text is designed to achieve, with a couple of tightly focussed objectives. Doing this before you start writing will remind you, for example, the questions your readers might have (and that you need to answer), the content you need to include, what evidence will persuade them, etc.

If you are writing a marketing leaflet to promote your services, decide whether your aim is to get them to visit your website, telephone you, complete and return a coupon, etc. And be prepared to challenge yourself. In this example, does the leaflet need to be tailored for a specific sector rather than a general leaflet for anyone, and how does that affect your language? How will you stand out from your competitors (e.g. via testimonials, location, or price/service promises)? And what content or techniques can you use to nudge people into contacting you?

Know your audience, i.e. who you are writing for

When taking out a newspaper/magazine advertisement, compiling a webpage or leaflet, etc., it's easy to be tempted to describe *all our services* – so that we maximise our chances of a 'hit' or sale. After all, the cost of advertising and printing can soon mount up, and restricting one's offer to only some services, or only some markets/audiences, would seem fool-hardy – and potentially expensive.

The danger of this approach is that such a leaflet runs the risk of *not fitting any of your target markets*, and as a result you don't get any hits at all. In most cases you might therefore be better to concentrate on writing for a particular target market – which will require getting to know about them beforehand, and writing specifically with them in mind. (This is the difference between general marketing and more specific selling.)

Different markets will vary considerably, and the headings and buzzwords you use, plus how you persuade potential customers to buy, etc. will vary according to the following customer details:

◆ Gender, age and background

◆ Location

◆ Sector

◆ Prior knowledge of your product/service

◆ Drivers and motivators

◆ Reservations and concerns

◆ Affordability

◆ Time factors.

Are they ready to buy?

Your language might also vary according to your audience's attitude to buying new products. Are they: innovators and early adopters (who might be persuaded by words such as 'new' and 'exciting'); more like the majority of the population (who will prefer things that are tried and tested, and will want supporting evidence); or late adopters (who are more risk averse, and will need reassuring).

Attract readers' interest

Tapping into people's emotions is the best way to persuade people, and to sell things. Businesses know this very well, so their advertisements don't concentrate solely on their products' features (e.g. *3½-feet wide computer table, with sliding drawers*), or their advantages (e.g. *Specially designed for computer work/equipment*), but on the benefits to the customer ('*The professional choice that is easy to work with*' and '*Get your desk job done right away*' – both of which are from IKEA's website). Charities also do this, tapping into our emotions when getting us to donate money.

And just think about the last time you went to the cinema. All those car advertisements, for example, barely talk about the *features* of the cars at all; instead they focus on their maker's brand, the particular car's image, the terrains the cars can cope with, and the dream-like places they will take you to.

Using emotions to attract readers

◆ **'Explore new places'** (much more intriguing than what could have just been 'guided holidays to' China)

◆ **'Part Urban Dweller, Part Country Getaway'** (relates well to the lifestyle and aspirations of purchasers of the sports cars that were pictured beneath it)

◆ **'Take it all in your stride'** (attracts those who like walking holidays, and underlines Jersey's easy reach – no stressful, long-distance travel required to get there)

◆ **'Polar Proof'** (suggests that wearers of the jacket that was pictured below will be as warm and wrapped up as polar bears).

SOURCE: Advertisement headlines

When selling to businesses

However, when selling to businesses your text will need to be different. Whereas *consumers* are swayed by benefits (explained above), *businesses* may want more objective details. This is because most people in business will need to: get approval from/or persuade several people to go ahead, justify the cost to someone, and be confident your product/service will fit into their brand.

Another way of looking at selling to business is that they need to know if your product/service is going to reduce their costs, increase their profits – or maybe even advance the decision-maker's career.

Connecting with readers

Once you have got a good feel for your audience, and how to attract their interest, here are some more subtle techniques to help you with your writing:

◆ **Headlines** – there is nothing more effective, and fundamental, than having good headlines. Think how much difference good headlines can make to email subject lines, advertising copy and newspaper/magazine billboards.

  Here are some ideas for wording your headlines, in these cases related to helping people improve their website. For example, show how to do something (*Quick tips to boost your website*), explain something (*Reasons your website may not perform well*), be provocative (*We bet your website can do better*), use numbers (*8 Ways to boost your website*), issue an invitation (*Join our web expert's mailing list*), make an offer (*£200 discount on our website training*), use questions (*Are you satisfied with your website?*), use a testimonial, use an analogy or metaphor, adapt a film/song title, be teasing, use a pun, etc., etc.

◆ **I/we and you** – using the first personal pronoun (I/we) and second (you) creates more engaging text than when using the third (he, she or it), which can sound impersonal, unfriendly and distant.

◆ **Emotions** – you can stir people into acting by tapping into their emotions/drivers such as greed, envy, fear, pride, guilt, excitement, hope, etc.

◆ **Use a story** – an obvious way to catch people's attention is through a direct approach that calls their attention (e.g. *Don't Miss Out....*). But telling them a story is also effective. Also, it should enable you to hold their attention for longer – which will be useful when writing lengthier pieces of text such as some brochures, webpages and blogs.

◆ **Be personal** – at the end of the day we are all humans, and so we relate best to one other. So being a bit personal in your document (which doesn't mean revealing private confidences) can be a really effective way to connect with your reader. Look at how internet blogs do this. Depending on what you are writing, revealing a bit of your personality, and maybe some of your interests, habits and personal situation, creates an image of someone that readers can imagine and relate to.

Motivational phrases

Motivational phrases can also stir readers into action and you may be able to adapt or draw on the everyday ones around you, such as the following:

- *Because you're worth it* [L'Oreal]

- *You shop, we drop* [Tesco]

- *It could be you* [National Lottery]

- *Refreshes the parts that other beers cannot reach* [Heineken]

- *Don't you deserve the best!*

- *You know what you want, so go for it.*

- *Resistance is futile. Go on!*

Psychological triggers

At the start of this chapter I mentioned that people are swayed by psychological influences (as well as just good writing), and that you will need to weave these into your text. The web can provide you with more details of this, but here are some ideas to start you off, with examples.

- People like to feel they are part of a group (*Clearly, you're someone who cares about…*).

- They don't like to miss out (use time-limited offers and bargains).

- They are swayed by comparisons (show how your product/ service is cheaper or better than an alternative).

◆ You can steer people to buying one product/service by citing another, more costly alternative.

◆ Make them feel happy and your product/service seem fun; then they are more likely to say 'Yes'.

◆ Given the choice between equal items, people are more likely to choose the item that is last in a list.

The power of repetition

Repetition can help you emphasise and get a message across, and I think it is underused in copywriting. Don't forget all the different types of repetition you can do. For example, repetition of particular words/phrases ('*Location, location, location*'), of a given sentence structure ('*I came, I saw, I conquered*'), or repetition at either the start or end of phrases ('*Dream it, Believe it, Achieve it.*'), etc.

> **Key Point:** Politicians and other speech givers use repetition a lot, and you too might find this effective (e.g. Obama's '*Yes we can...*', Martin Luther King's '*I have a dream...*', etc.). But be careful; if the word/phrase is overused, or unfamiliar to the audience, it can grate on them (e.g. *One Nation, Big Society, hard-working families*, etc.).

When writing proposals

Sometimes the task of persuading people may be more difficult. You may have to overcome their customs and beliefs, objections and reservations, biases and prejudices, etc. (Anyone who has to persuade children to do things will know what I mean – if this doesn't apply to you, listen to the techniques of a good showroom salesman.)

This is particularly true when writing proposals, and especially if your suggestions are more costly, lengthy, or against the trend. But it can be done with the following tips:

- ◆ Be reasonable; don't be dismissive of their views.

- ◆ Use research evidence to support your ideas.

- ◆ Can you use any references and testimonials to support your case?

- ◆ Make suggestions that are easy and simple for them to adopt.

- ◆ Think how to counter people's opposition and concerns.

- ◆ Don't be personal when rejecting others' views – instead, find reasons that make it easier for them to back down, and to accept your solution, such as 'changes in circumstances', or 'opportunities from new technology', etc.

Further reading

FT Essential Guide to Business Writing: How to Write to Engage, Persuade and Sell – Ian Atkinson. Pearson, 2012.

Persuasive Writing – Peter Frederick. Pearson, 2011.

Practice writing exercises

Collect around ten advertisements that you think are good, from newspapers and magazines etc. Then decide which ones you think have the best main headings, and why. Ask someone else to look through the advertisements, and see if their views are the same as yours. Discuss any differences – bear in mind different people are influenced and persuaded by different things, so you may not necessarily agree.

Are any 'psychological triggers' (such as those on p. 90) used in the advertisements you have collected above. Which ones work best, and why? Ask someone else to look through the advertisements, and see if their views are the same as yours. Discuss any differences – bear in mind different people are influenced and persuaded by different things, so you may not necessarily agree.

One way of engaging your readers is by telling a story – using characters (maybe yourself), a plot and a message. Write a short story (under 200 words) about your company/organisation, focussing e.g. on people/a person you helped, the best things you do, etc.

List the main reasons why you think some people might be reluctant to buy your products or services. For each of the reasons, use the ideas on pp. 91–2 to come up responses that might persuade people to buy. Should you work any of these into your advertising, marketing, website, etc.?

Make a note of any 'motivating phrases' (as p. 90) that you find persuasive – from shops, advertisements, billboards, in cinemas, etc. Can you work any of these into your advertising, marketing, website, etc.?

Part 4

Writing for Particular Outputs

10

Improve your website

- Homepages
- Straplines
- Write for 'scannability'
- Catch readers' attention – Slow them down
- Be user-focussed
- How to structure your web text
- Front-load your content
- About Us webpages
- When several people write your web text
- Test your text in print

"One involves reading paper, the other involves reading light.**"**

(A comparison of reading printed content versus reading online content.)

Garth Bucholz

Websites are important, but writing for them is not quite the same as 'normal' writing. No, it's not as hard as learning a foreign language, but there are some subtle differences. So I hope what follows is useful advice.

Homepages

Your homepage is important but be careful of overloading it with too much content. Yes, it is tempting to put there lots of things you are proud of – and colleagues may be badgering you to post *their* stories as well – but the more content you have, the more each message is diluted, and the less each's impact. It should be like a shop window: enticing people to come in (not overloaded), and then quickly directing them to the pages with the information they are looking for.

This point applies not just to your *overall homepage* but also to the other aspects of it: the length of your main headings; the titles of news stories, pictures and messages on your 'carousel' (the changing images at the top); your straplines (the words you put alongside your logo, e.g. *You shop, We drop*); etc.

Homepages should be about making a few strong and short messages to your readers, but too often I see good messages drowned out by too much content. Remember 'Less is more.'

Also on your homepage should be a clear, one-sentence, jargon-free summary of what you do – something that people can quote to others, use in a press release, etc. Here is an example, from one of the delegates on my training courses: *The Gurkha Welfare Trust is the leading Gurkha welfare charity. We provide financial, medical and community aid to alleviate hardship and distress among Gurkha ex-servicemen of the British Crown.*

You'd be amazed how often I find homepages that don't spell out clearly what the business or organisation does.

Straplines

Many organisations and businesses have a slogan or 'strapline' – a sentence or two that represents their ethos or way of working. Some you will be familiar with are Tesco's *Every Little Helps*, BMW's *The Ultimate Driving Machine*, and Nike's *Just Do It*.

What about you? It may be just a short phrase, e.g. *Your one-stop guide to Oxford Life*, or a few adjectives that describe your product/service, e.g. *Principled, Reliable and Honest.* Either way, it's probably something that you are proud of, often recite to customers, and spent a while preparing.

Now, if I *visit* your organisation/business I am pretty sure I would come away without knowing whether or not you had such a slogan. But supposing you do have one, are you making the most of it? And in particular, is it on your website – where it can be really prominent, and where it can reach far more people than hung behind your Reception.

> **Key Point:** If you are tempted by this idea of having a strapline somewhere prominent on your website, there is no need to spend 12 months, or a fortune, getting it drawn up. And for goodness sake don't devalue its impact (as I see sometimes) by putting it in a small typeface, or crowding it out with other, less important information.

Write for 'scannability'

With most readers *scanning* your web text rather than reading all of it (research suggests most users only read 20–30 per cent), it's not the place for 'indulgent' writing – and for those who enjoy writing, this might come as a frustration. (Some people call writing for the web 'painful', as it means stripping text down to its bare bones.)

Instead of spending time writing beautiful prose, with lovely descriptions, subtle punctuation, etc. (which is fine for writing fiction, feature articles and case studies), what matters is whether your text stands out, and is *quick and easy to read.* In a word, maximise your text's 'scannability' – not a beautiful word, but you know what I mean. For example, the web is the place for short sentences and short paragraphs.

Like this.

Key Point: There are lots of ways to help your page's scannability. For example, write clear headings; include images/graphics; use large font sizes, quotes and sub-headings; and best of all ... use bullet points, which work wonders. When used correctly (i.e. don't have too many in a group, or not without a sub-heading) they work like magnets, pulling in readers' attention – which is of course what you want.

Write for scannability

PSYCHOMETRIC TESTING AND PERSONALITY PROFILES

Psychometric testing is now a fundamental part of recruitment. Everyday more companies are integrating it as part of their process in getting the right people for the job.

WHAT IS A PSYCHOMETRIC TEST?

It is a device that is used to find out about individual differences: personal characteristics, underlying actions, possible future behaviour, how 'good' you are at something compared with other groups of people.

There are two main kinds of psychometric test:

◆ **Skills tests** measure how well you do something, and are split into ability and aptitude tests.

◆ **Ability tests** can include numerical, verbal, and logical reasoning, problem-solving skills, and the ability to identify mistakes accurately.

◆ **Aptitude tests** assess your ability to use specific job-related skills, and predict future performance. They examine your potential to learn to do a new task rather than testing the skills you already have.

◆ **Personality tests** measure less quantifiable characteristics – they reveal your motivation, attitude & work style. For a retail sales role, for example, the company may want someone who is very sociable, organised and creative.

COMMENTS: Some very scannable text thanks to clear sections, short paragraphs, a few short bullet points and the use of bold. Questions are also a good way to engage the reader, and in this case ask the question many readers might have. The very clear and straight to the point writing style also helps. However, the page isn't perfect. 'Two' psychometric tests is confusing. Also, CAPITALS are harder to scan, so I usually discourage them; but these aren't too long and provide another type of heading.

SOURCE: Start of webpage on psychometric testing from www.mccarthyrecruitment.com. (I deleted a couple of sentences to make the extract fit.)

Catch readers' attention – Slow them down

In addition to writing for scannability, I recommend tweaking your text so that it maximises your chances of catching readers' attention. Here are four tips you may not have seen elsewhere:

- **Numbers** – By convention we write in words small numbers up to ten or eleven (it varies between publishers and organisations' style guidelines) and use digits for any numbers that are greater. However, digits stand out more to the eye than words, so using digits may be better for *all* numbers on the web (e.g. *3 Reasons to Choose us*).

- **Use questions** – Writing headings/sub-headings as questions can quite often get the reader to stop and think about what you have written. It is as though they have some secret power, making the reader pause and think, 'Um, what is my answer to that?'

- **Abbreviate your sentences** – There is no need to write grammatically correct sentences in your headings/sub-headings. Far more eye-catching to readers will be the sort of language you see in adverts or billboards: e.g. *Beware traffic*, not *Please beware of the traffic*. Or, '*Give 'em a Spin*', which, as I write, is the homepage of the cleaning products company, Method.

- **Language** – The web can be impersonal, but if you use the first and second person pronouns (I/we and you) rather than the third (your company name, or he/she/it) your text will have more of a 'voice', and engage better with your readers. For example, *We invite you to visit* our *offices* compared to *Company ABC invites customers to visit its offices.*

Be user-focussed

It is very easy to sit down and, without thinking, write about something *from the way we see it* as opposed to the perspective that *readers want to know about it*. For example, a business/organisation may describe itself on its About Us page using *its* departmental structure/headings, even though these may not make sense or represent the names of services where people are looking for help.

On the web it means thinking through the purpose-driven nature of most readers, what is sometimes called their 'Grab and Go' mentality (i.e. they are searching for something specific and don't want to hang around). Ask yourself, Who are your website's readers, What do they want, and What does that require from you? Taken one step further, think of answering why they should use you rather than others.

Councils have got pretty good at this. When I worked at one in the 1990s the three main departments were called Education, Highways and Leisure Services. Today the same departments are more likely to be called Schools and Learning; Roads and Transport; Heritage, Culture and Recreation – which are far more meaningful, and will be speedier at channelling readers to the webpage they need.

Good website navigation really helps

Managing a large website, such as councils have to, is quite a challenge – getting people to the page they want, answering their query, and keeping information up to date. Enabling people to navigate around such large websites is key.

Councils have realised that the overwhelming majority of queries to their websites can be put under just four headings (as below, with examples of services). However, variations on this are sometimes needed. For example, in tourist areas such as the Isle of Wight the council homepage's main headings are Residents, Businesses and Visitors.

- ◆ **Report it** – pot holes, pavements, bins, traffic signals, street lighting.
- ◆ **Apply for it** – Blue Badges, bus pass, school admissions, waste permit.
- ◆ **Pay for it** – Council Tax, penalties, fees, fines, rents, debts.
- ◆ **Book it** – library computer, home fire safety visit, register a birth.

COMMENTS: These headings are great for councils' homepages: they are short (so don't need much space), and very clear and simple (it's easy to realise where queries will answered), so they get people quickly to the page they want. Are there any lessons for simplifying your website's navigation?

How to structure your web text

If you have ever written a press release you will know that journalists are taught to structure their news stories in the shape of 'an inverted pyramid'. Let me explain this first, and then I'll tell you the relevance for writing for the web.

The inverted pyramid shape means that a news story has the *most* amount of content at its start (the wide base of a pyramid inverted, turned upside down), where it tells readers the five W's that people typically want to know about a news story: Who has done What; When and Where did it happen; and Why. And the story gradually thins out, with less and less *new* content towards the end (represented by the pyramid's narrowing peak, when turned upside down). This is true of news stories in newspapers and magazines, and even more so of radio and TV, where listeners can't re-read a journalist's first sentence/paragraph for clarification.

So what, you might ask. Well, research shows that the amount of content people read decreases as they move down any given webpage (nearly everyone reads the headlines, but very few get to the foot of the page), which means you should write in this inverted pyramid format, with all your key content in the first few paragraphs.

So, the start of my website's copywriting page is: 'Need some text written? Rewriting your website? Want to start a blog? I can write your brochure, case study, newsletter.'

In contrast, blogs (and newspaper/magazine features) should be structured like a diamond. Let me explain. Their introduction should have only a little content, but one that hooks the reader, for example with a fact, beautiful description or intriguing sentence. All the detail of the story appears later on, somewhere around the middle – i.e. where the diamond is at its widest – and the story narrows towards the end, e.g. with a summarising comment, or quote.

Here's an example of an intriguing introduction for a diamond shape – the start of a blog I wrote for the Thames Valley networking group, MD2MD: *NERDS may be the subject of jokes, but there is nothing wrong with being one in business. In fact, being a nerd may be GOOD for your business. And here's how…*

Front-load your content

We read from left to right, so it can be helpful to position strong, eye-catching words at the start of sentences/paragraphs so that they catch the readers' eye as they scroll down the left margin. And that may mean rewording some of your sentences. Let me explain.

We are taught to use the active tense/verb over the passive because it conveys momentum and results in shorter sentences – see below. The active is also more 'transparent', because you have to say *who* has done something, which you can hide or omit in a passive sentence. For example:

- *The committee wrote a damning report* [active tense/verb – 6 words]

- *A damning report has been written by the committee* [passive tense/verb – 9 words, although '*by the committee*' is optional]

The passive tense is identified by usage of the past participle of the main verb (here, 'written'), preceded by part of an auxiliary verb (to have/to be/to get; in this case 'has been').

Now, the sentence starting with *A damning report* will be more eye-catching than the other. So, despite the normal advice to use the active tense, on the web the passive may work better.

About Us webpages

Websites can be impersonal. 'Any old Joe' can put up a website and claim to deliver a service, provide what you are looking for, or be the answer to your problems. But before we make contact or hand over any cash most of us would like to know a bit more … Who is Joe, How long has he been in business, and Why should I put my faith in *him* over other companies on the web?

So, your About Us webpage (and there is no need to call it anything else) is an opportunity to stand out from your competition. Avoid soulless corporate speak, jargon and what readers might see as predictable business values. Rhubarb, rhubarb; bla, bla, bla. Tell us something real, genuine and original – that gets behind the 'front' that some organisations present to the public.

Some interesting About Us pages I have seen have had a pictorial timeline of the business, a photo of the founder or previous premises (best in black and white), a story of how/why they went into business (signed at the bottom for effect and to make them personal), etc.

Here's an example of an About Us that is a bit different, and that has a good voice.

An effective 'About Us' webpage

We've been making impeccably stylish, beautifully designed products, principally in white, for over 20 years. Think style not fashion, quality not quantity and an attention to detail that extends through everything we do – from the hand-stitching on a luxurious high thread-count pillowcase to our second-to-none customer service…. I cannot emphasize enough how much love, care and attention to detail goes into every item we make.

COMMENTS: The colourful and original language ('impeccably stylish … luxurious high thread-count pillowcase') conveys a really special product, with overtones of helping us to sleep peacefully. Every possible customer wish is mentioned ('attention to detail … hand-stitching … second-to-none customer service'), and the lovely balanced rhythms ('Think style not fashion, quality not quantity … love, care and attention to detail') emphasise key messages.

SOURCE: The White Company, www.thewhitecompany.com

When several people write your web text

If several people write content for one website, and in particular if you have to edit others' text, it is worth having a *short* web writing style-guide – to have a consistent writing style, reduce the time an editor spends editing, etc. Let me explain.

Most people are familiar with styleguides as something that specifies the exact colours and design of an organisation's/company's logo. But newspapers, magazines and book publishers use styleguides to remind their journalists, authors and contributors of their in-house conventions. For example, a styleguide will have advice and listings on: how to write acronyms (UN as opposed to U.N. or United Nations); formatting (per cent not percent in text, but use % in tables); reminders of word meanings (principal versus principle) and spellings preferences (usage not useage); etc.

Key Point: So, if several people write text for your website, a styleguide to steer their writing should help. It only needs to be a few pages, and you can draw it up with colleagues. (It you want ideas, you will find some examples on the web.) It might cover, for example, spelling and other conventions (as above); you might decide on a maximum sentence and paragraph length; and you can include the formatting characteristics of websites whose styles you like (e.g. the BBC's practice of putting a webpage's first paragraph in bold); etc. If you get it signed off by your senior manager, and circulated, it will provide a handy reference for staff and reduce the workload of your website's editor.

Test your text in print

What do we do when we *really* want to read something, or check something? Print it out – exactly! But how many of us print out our *webpages* when we want to review or finalise them? If you do, I guarantee you will spot things you didn't before. You'll even ask yourself, 'How did I miss that?'

Further reading

Don't Make Me Think! – Seth Godin. New Riders Publishing, 2006.

My blog. Available at: www.perfecttext.org/blog/

The Big Red Fez. How to Make Any Web Site Better – Seth Godin. Simon & Schuster, 2002.

Writing for the Web – Susannah Ross. Chambers Harrap Publishers, 2007.

Practice writing exercises

Write a possible strapline (a sentence or set of words) that encapsulates your business/organisation. Even if it is only a draft, try out the effect of placing it somewhere prominent on your website. Decide if it is an idea worth pursuing.

Print out one of your longest webpages, ideally one at least 500 words. Now imagine you only have half the space available, so reduce the text by around 50 per cent. Also take into account the need for the text to be as scannable as possible. Try putting this different and shorter content on the original webpage. Are there any lessons for having shorter content on any of your other webpages?

For your website's homepage and any other key webpages, see if you can catch readers' attention and slow them down more with any of the ideas for headings on p. 101.

Examine the 'About Us' page (or equivalent) on your website. At the very minimum it should be: (a) clear and informative; (b) an interesting read, e.g. by telling the story or background to your business/organisation; and (c) make you stand out/be different from your competitors. Edit your text to improve it where necessary – it should only take an hour or so, but you might need to collate some material first.

Make sure the headlines to your website's news stories are as short as possible (five or six words maximum). Any longer and they will hide their main message and not stand out to readers.

Tips for case studies, features and blogs

- Follow the classic structure
- Be topical
- Remind yourself of your audience
- Look for an angle/hook
- Write a grabbing introduction
- Be a pleasure to read
- Be specific – Use a case study
- Get a good quote
- Have a good ending
- Edit, edit, edit

" The way a story is written must match the subject, the mood and pace of the events described and, above all, the needs of the reader. "

Wynford Hicks

If you enjoy writing, then this chapter is for you. For while the structure to webpages, reports and press releases is fairly rigid, you have much more freedom when writing case studies, features and blogs. Indeed, in journalism it is often said that the only constraint to writing features is to write in a way that is right for your audience and publication. (That is why I loved feature writing for newspapers; and being freelance I also got to choose my own subjects.)

But what makes a *really good* case study or blog? Like news stories, they should inform their readers, but they should also, for example, entertain, tell a story, persuade and influence readers, and be an enjoyable read. Here are a few tips to get you on the way.

Follow the classic structure

Features are traditionally structured in a diamond shape – the width representing the amount of content. Let me explain. At the start your text should be focussed on grabbing the readers' interest (the narrow top of a diamond); only once you have sucked readers in do you give them all the details of what you are writing about (the widest part of the diamond); and you end your feature with a neat summary/conclusion, which may be captured for example in a quote (the narrow base of the diamond).

You can follow the same format for blogs and case studies, although for the latter you may want to adopt a more traditional structure, like: What was the problem / What we did / What was the outcome. I know, those sub-headings are not very original; but if people are appraising you and your business/organisation they are looking for answers to those questions, so it's in your interest to 'serve them on a plate'.

Be topical

Most of us are exposed to a very powerful media several times a day, telling us the day's 'hard news' stories (what is on the front page of newspapers), but also all the other 'soft news' stories (about what else is going on e.g. in the arts, entertainment and sport).

Now, readers *need a reason* to read your case study, feature or blog. Yes, you can write on any old thing and hope they notice it, but your work has far more chance of being read and noticed if it is on a topical subject – if it is linked to one of the hard or soft news stories above, or is something that everyone is talking about. Ideally it wants to link to those stories, but be a different angle on them, which gives the reader the reason for reading it. And it may be particularly powerful if you can make the link in your heading.

> **Key Point:** To see how to hang content on a news hook, and its benefits, tune into one of your local radio stations. Now, their goal is to get local people listening, and talking about what they have heard with their friends. So, they sometimes take a story in the national news, which is in their listeners' minds, and do their own angle on it, to get people to phone into their programmes. For example, as I write it's October 2014 and a jogger on his way to the gym has accidentally run into the Prime Minister, David Cameron. So what did BBC Radio Oxford do? It ran a phone-in inviting people to share famous people they have 'bumped into' (or not recognised, etc.).

Remind yourself of your audience

It is easy to forget sometimes *who* we are writing for. We can get so carried away with the job of writing – excited by the invitation to submit something, the prospect of our work being printed and our services/products promoted – that we write *from our perspective*, rather than *focussing on our audience*: who are they and what do they want from reading our text. (There is more on this in Chapter 3.)

If you think about it, how you promote a product/service in a business magazine will be very different from a newspaper article; and what you write on a LinkedIn group for small businesses will be very different from a community newsletter, etc. – or *it should be*.

I made this mistake once when I got a commission to write a magazine feature on a chef, her life story and new cookbook. Visiting her smallholding and restaurant (and getting a taste or two) made the research very enjoyable; and writing about an interesting lady, and her beautiful estate, made the writing easy – or so I thought.

Part of the article was a 200-word cooking tip for readers. But I forgot that the magazine's readers (the *Caterer and Hotelkeeper*) weren't the newspaper readers I usually wrote for, but, as the editor reminded me after I submitted my article, *professional chefs* who wanted original ways to cook, and were happy with highly practical ideas. It was a little embarrassing as I had to ring the chef again, collect a more suitable cooking tip from her (we ended up with 'How to cure bacon'), and the extra work meant I didn't earn much for the job – although I did get a copy of her great cookbook.

Look for an angle/hook

The challenge of writing features and blogs is not explaining what you know – or shouldn't be, because that should be relatively straightforward. Instead, it is about finding an angle, hook or way of telling it that will be really engaging and attract the interest of as many of your target audience as possible. That is your goal: to look for that 'inspiration in the shower' moment. I liken it to doing the Rubik's cube: playing around with what you have until you suddenly see a way that will work best for your readers.

Here is an example you might enjoy. One cold December day I gave a training course in blogging to some highly knowledgeable solicitors and accountants – experts in VAT, corporation tax, employment law, etc. Blogging was not their favourite activity, especially when I told them they had 15 minutes to write one. But they wrote some great blogs, hanging many of them on the seasonal theme that was all around us, which increased the chances of their blogs being read. It was several years ago, but I still remember how one blog was about Santa checking his contracts of employment for all his reindeer. It was brilliant, and we all laughed. The author had found a perfect angle/hook. So, the hook doesn't have to be a news story, it can be a season, an analogy, popular sports or common hobbies, a situation facing many readers, etc.

Write a grabbing introduction

One of the most important requirements of a good feature is to have a really grabbing introduction. Since your aim is to get the reader to read your *whole piece*, you entice them in with a few details/sentences, gradually telling them more, only putting the detailed stuff around the middle of the text, and neatly summarise things or coming to a conclusion at the end. But that first sentence, that first paragraph, needs to be really really strong.

Think about the last time you heard a good talk at a conference, saw a good film, or read a good book. It's likely that the start was really impressive: maybe it grabbed you, presented a story, took you to another place, was beautifully written, shocked you, etc. That's the sort of thing you need to achieve with the start of your feature, case study or blog.

Chapter 6 has some ideas for good introductions, and Chapter 2 stresses there is no need to *begin* your writing there. Better to leave writing it until later, when you know what is going to follow it.

Be a pleasure to read

All features should be readable, accurate, topical, credible, etc., but they should also be a pleasure for the audience to read. Here are some ingredients they should contain:

- ◆ Flowing text, easy to read
- ◆ Strong storyline, maybe with twists or an element of surprise
- ◆ Play on words
- ◆ Good rhythm (based on word sounds, sentence length, etc.)
- ◆ A recurring theme e.g. repeated use of a particular colour
- ◆ Satisfying conclusion, e.g. returning to the theme of the start.

Working one or more of these into your feature will make it a more enjoyable and memorable read.

Be specific – Use a case study

When writing any kind of marketing material, you might be tempted to describe how your product/service can be used by all kinds of people, in all kinds of situations. You might even have some aggregate data such as '76% of readers described our Investor Magazine as "excellent",' or '65% of businesses said our project planning toolkit increased their profitability.' Useful data, and sounds good. But readers will relate best to, and probably be more influenced by, individual, named examples and specific case studies.

> **Key Point:** As people we relate best to stories, case studies and anecdotes of one another, which people can identify with better than aggregate data. So, do everything you can to collect attributable quotes and testimonials, and demonstrate your work capabilities with specific examples, named case studies, etc.

Here's an example of being specific, from a testimonial on my website: 'We wanted to introduce new styles of writing. Robert's training was a perfect blend of theoretical and practical, and was thoroughly fascinating ... it helped us apply different styles to the variety of publications we use, from formal briefs to our less formal magazine articles.' – Louise Simpson. Evidence Director, Army Families Federation.

For here and 'Get a good quote' (below), you might find it a lot faster if *you* draft something for your client to approve. People can have good intentions to help you, but sometimes are slow at getting round to it. It also means you can steer their comments to what aspects of your services you want them to comment on (e.g. price, service, delivery, etc.). If they disapprove of your draft, they can edit and amend as they see fit. (However, the testimonial above was unprompted – honest!)

Yes, collecting such case studies and examples can be tedious and take time to organise: contacting them, interviewing them, getting a good quote, asking their permission, etc. But these case studies needn't be long. And from my experience many people are happy to help – and you can always change their name if necessary.

Believe me, it'll be worth it.

Get a good quote

I have written elsewhere of the importance of having a good quote to liven up your writing and increase its impact (in Chapter 4) – which is equally true of features, case studies and blogs. A word of warning however…

Far too often I see quotes and testimonials (in particular in case studies and on websites) of eight to ten lines long. Eight to ten lines! Who wants to read one that long? Most readers won't have the appetite; they will glance over or ignore it, missing any key points. What you put so much effort into collecting is wasted.

Key Point: My advice is, don't be afraid *shorten* a long quote to get it to better suit your needs. (Obviously I don't mean shunting words around, but editing out the less important words. However, if you are re-ordering things, or want to do any other changes, you should get the person's approval.) So, get your red pen out, imagine yourself as a journalist who only has limited space, and extract the really pithy, most congratulatory and informative words.

Have a good ending

Reading can be a pleasurable experience, and anything of any length needs to be – to keep the reader turning the pages. The structure should be clear, the 'story' or content should move along, there should be variety and quotes to keep it alive, and maybe a surprise or two to keep the reader guessing.

And one more ingredient that will tickle any reader is a nice, clear ending. What do I mean? One that, for example – and depending what you are writing – goes back to the beginning of your story, wraps things up, looks ahead, identifies prospects and possibilities for the future, draws some conclusions or recommendations, that sort of thing.

Usually, I don't have any difficulty finding a good *ending* to a piece – indeed, I often spot it early on. They are often a quote by someone, whose words neatly summarise everything I have been writing about. It's the *beginning* that I sometimes struggle with, and I often only write much later on, when I know what text will follow it.

Somehow, a good ending makes reading the piece so much more satisfying. It's comforting; it leaves the reader feeling warm and content; it puts a smile on their face.

Examples of possible endings

Summarise – 'So, self-builders get profit, the environment gets a more eco-friendly property, and our landscape gets a distinctive home.'

Concluding quote – '"It's a cast-iron rule that where parents are really behind the school, their children always do well."'

Repeat the most important point(s) – 'The most critical thing is to continue the debate and it's a debate that ministers and civil servants need to engage in fully.'

Provoke readers – 'Every countryman and woman must take up that responsibility. It's time to insist. Let battle commence.'

Outline future prospects/possibilities – 'It all suggests that there are a few more chapters left in this fairy tale yet.'

SOURCE: Original articles, in my training notes

Edit, edit, edit

Chapter 16 gives more details of the importance of revising, editing and proofreading, and how best to do them. Together, I suggest they will take you around 25–40 per cent of the total time you spend working on a job. But here are three tips specific to editing case studies, features and blogs.

- ◆ Double-check the usefulness of your first couple of paragraphs – Inexperienced writers often start a feature/blog with introductory passages to set the scene, etc., but they are not necessary. In fact, deleting them often makes the piece much better.

- Give yourself a target page length/word count – This forces you to check that every sentence and phrase (every word, even) is absolutely necessary to your text, i.e. that it adds or explains something. Look out for any waffle/unnecessary words and phrases.

- I find that printing out my work, and using a red pen, helps me take on the role of editor, and helps ensure I am critical of my own text.

- Read your work out loud – This should help you spot where, for example, the narrative is flagging, the sentences are too long, or there are too many sentences of similar length, producing a monotonous rhythm, etc.

Further reading

Writing for journalists – Wynford Hicks. Routledge, 2008

Practice writing exercises

Tune into your local BBC radio station on a few different days, listening out for the subjects they choose for their phone-in and discussion programmes. As described on p. 111, radio stations are very good at using stories in the national news as hooks for their own programmes. Listening to what hooks they use may give you some ideas for your writing.

Take a glance at some different kinds of writing – newspapers, magazines, webpages, blogs, etc. – and note whether their introductions follow the inverted triangle shape (of news stories and webpages) or the diamond (as in case studies, features and blogs). Have you got your introductions right?

As a follow-up exercise to the above, decide which of the diamond-shaped introductions (a structure that allows a lot of variety within in) you like, and why. What ideas do they give you for your writing?

Read the testimonials and other quotes on your brochures, webpages, etc. Check they are clear, not too long and are powerful, etc. If any are more than two sentences/lines, see if shortening them increases their impact with readers.

12

Increase your report's impact

"By failing to prepare you are preparing to fail."
Benjamin Franklin

Reports can make or break a project, a funding decision, and an organisation's or person's reputation. But they don't come out of thin air. If you want a really good one it needs advance planning, accurate data collection, and good writing-up and editing skills.

What – and why – are you writing?

Some reports have a very clear purpose, which means you can get started straight away. But this is not always the case. For example, the reason for your report may not be written down anywhere; people may be saying different things about it (in terms of their expectations, its coverage and usage); and you may be on the sidelines of the organisation/group that commissioned it, so are/feel remote from discussions that led to it.

As author, it is essential you are rock solid on all of the following, which may mean postponing your start until you are more confident. Make sure you have clear answers.

◆ Have you clear, written objectives?

◆ Check who the report is for – if there are multiple audiences, how will they be served?

◆ When is it due?

◆ Are there any strong views on its content, data sources and format?

◆ Are people looking for answers to particular questions, for policy recommendations, etc.?

◆ Check the goalposts have not moved since the report was first commissioned.

Who is your report for?

When planning your report, collecting data and writing it, you should pause to think a little about the nature and any specific requirements of your audience. If you take into account their needs, biases and preferences – and you may have more than one group to consider – you will improve your chances of getting your message across. Here are a few things you should reflect upon, about the audience:

◆ Their background, interest and time available to read the report

◆ Knowledge of/Views on the subject

◆ Preferences towards any particular kinds of data, or data sources

◆ Sections of greatest interest

◆ Sections they may find difficult/have little knowledge of

◆ Likely views/reactions to your findings

◆ Personal preferences – report's length, format, types of data, etc.

Remember that some external consultants' reports are commissioned in order to justify a decision that has already been taken (or at least in people's heads), so check what precisely is the reason for the report and what results does the client want to see/read.

Don't start too early

When faced with a big job such as writing a report, one can be tempted to feel 'the sooner I start the better' – after all, there is less now to be done. But as explained above, when it comes to writing reports it is essential to know first exactly what you are writing, why and who for – all of which can influence your content.

Yes, getting started can seem a good idea – a page written, something ticked off, and some momentum gained – but the chances are that you will have to edit or rewrite it to reflect things you learn later on.

Still tempted to get started early on? My advice is don't!

On a related point, it might seem strange but don't write the introduction until you have written all the rest. This is so that if reflects the *final content* rather than what you think, when you start, will be the content (see also Chapter 2).

Planning the research

A key part of any report is its data: the evidence it uses to support its case. So a key early stage for you will be to plan the following: what data do you need, does any new data need to be collected (primary data), where can other data be found (secondary data), who is going to do the research, and how long will it take to collect and analyse.

Take it from me, collecting data – in particular any that you are going to collect yourself – often takes longer than you expect, especially once you include time for checking, analysing, looking at other sources, deciding how best to present it, etc.

You may be able to start writing parts of your report while your data collection and other research continues. However, other parts will be totally dependent on the data, so don't start these before you know what story the data tells.

Whatever you do, allow enough time for your research.

Go for visual impact

As you do your research you should come across (or manage to collect yourself) some data, quotes, figures, etc., that will *really help* your report – that will make your case far far better than umpteen pages of text. You probably know what I mean: 'killer facts' that the media would jump on, that are so telling that they will be branded around at a committee meeting, and/or that would convince even your most ardent of opponents.

Remember, 'A picture is worth a thousand words'. So can be a figure. And diagrams, if you have to explain something complex.

My most memorable experience of this was when trying to make the case that parts of Shropshire deserved the same European funding – to support low-income hill farmers – as neighbouring mid Wales. We collected endless data on farm incomes, population density and lack of services, but were having difficulty convincing EU officials ... until we presented them with a satellite picture showing the two regions' undeniable common *geography* (and hence socio-economic conditions), which gave them a convincing case for their funding to straddle the England–Wales border.

> **Key Point:** You should be able to think of one or two killer facts for your report – maybe even before you start writing. It is worth doing everything you can to collect them, and thinking carefully how best to present them. They will be worth their weight in gold and help you achieve your report's objectives.

Don't underestimate the final stages

However long it takes you to *write* your report – a few days or weeks, or several months – my experience is that we all underestimate how long it will take to do the final ten per cent, i.e. to get it *completely finished*.

It's only natural to write the easiest parts first – indeed, I'd actively encourage that – but invariably there will be little bits here and there that you left unfinished. And coming back to them later isn't just getting them written, it probably requires dealing with why they were not written in the first place, i.e. they may require more data, further thought, talking to someone else, etc. And that's not all. Most reports have tables, appendices, references and preliminary pages (lists of contents, tables, etc.) to be compiled at this stage as well.

> **Key Point:** Be careful of committing or announcing a premature date for your report's completion. Be prepared for a very bitty but highly necessary wrapping up stage, to get everything ready for publication.

Executive Summary/Conclusions

There's probably nothing more important to your report than its Executive Summary/Conclusions – and you shouldn't need me to tell you why. For example, it may be the only bit that some people read, some people may read it more than once, it may be shared with people beyond your main audience, and could be the focus of discussions at key meetings, etc.

To make an Executive Summary/Conclusions as good as possible the following ideas may help:

◆ Use a different typeface or other layout features to differentiate it.

◆ Make sure the first sentence is grabbing and engaging.

◆ Use bold text, bullet points and other features to emphasise your key points.

◆ Use the same main headings as in the report, and clear sub-headings to break up the text.

◆ Spell out any acronyms and explain any unfamiliar terms.

◆ Provide page references for those who want to read more details.

◆ Triple-check it for typos, etc.

◆ Make sure your summary, conclusions and recommendations are clear, and clearly reasoned.

Headings and sub-headings

Clear headings and sub-headings are a really important element to a report, not least so that the reader can find their way around easily. One technique you may have noticed in some reports, and I think works well, is to make a report's headings/sub-headings tell its story. So, instead of using generic headings/sub-headings like Introduction, Research findings, Conclusions, etc., try using headings/sub-headings that either summarise the sections, or use questions to engage with the reader. For example, Conclusions becomes 'What did we decide', and Next steps becomes 'What do we need to do now'. Framing your sections as questions will also help your *writing* – by nudging you into thinking, as you write, more about the reader, and answering these questions.

Here are the chapter's sub-headings of a report I helped with recently:

> <u>Calculating Your Sales Targets</u>
> What annual growth can I achieve?
> Put some strategic thinking into your marketing
> How many customers do I need?
> What if I don't have any other products to sell?

Editing reports

When writing long documents such as reports it is easy for some sections to become far longer than planned. This is especially true if lots of people are involved, and/or different people are compiling different sections, and only come together once finished. So, the editing stage is time to check your report's sections are about the right length, and that their relative length is right for the subject and your objectives, etc.

As a print journalist, nearly all of my writing had a maximum length to it, so I have got used to checking that each sentence and paragraph I write is critical or adds something of meaning or relevance to my text. You may have to do the same, for example if you want your Executive Summary to fit onto just one page.

Writing a short report can be harder than writing a long one, and you will need to make sure every paragraph counts.

> **Key Point:** One good editing practice is to check the start and end of each paragraph are really doing their job. The start of paragraphs should state clearly what they are about – and they may be written in bold to help those skimming through a report. The endings should recap anything complex, summarise that paragraph's discussion, or make any conclusions, etc.

Don't annoy your readers

When writing a report you don't usually face the length restrictions of other business writing, which would impose more discipline as you wrote, making you think whether every word in your text is accurate, needed and adds something.

So be careful, because without such pressures bad habits can sometimes creep into your writing. As you edit, keep an eye out for any of the following (a process I once saw wonderfully described as to 'Cut the flab'):

◆ woolly and unnecessary phrases (e.g. *It is interesting to note, Having therefore considered*)

◆ waffle (*It is my opinion that, Some people consider*)

◆ tautologies (*free gift, 4am in the morning*)

◆ unnecessary qualifiers (*quite, rather*)

◆ clichés (*at this moment in time, at the end of the day*)

◆ redundant words (*that, quite*), etc.

For readers of business writing, who have a choice as to whether or not to your read your text, such words and phrases are highly annoying – they slow them down, and make your text wordy, irritating and inaccurate. Be on guard as you edit.

Further reading

How to Write Reports and Proposals – Patrick Forsyth. Kogan Page, 2013.

Report Writing for Readers with Little Time – Rien Elling et al. Routledge, 2013.

The Plain English Campaign. Free guides. Special subjects – Reports. Available at: www.plainenglish.co.uk/free-guides.html

Practice writing exercises

Unless you are clear about the purpose of your report it is very unlikely that you will meet your objectives. Try completing this sentence for a recent/future report of yours: 'As a result of reading this report, the reader will…'. Doing this should help you focus your report on what is essential, and focus your mind as you write.

What are the various audiences for your next report? Identify their various characteristics as on p. 121, noting the implications for your report.

Looking back at the really key data, tables and diagrams in one of your recent reports (or predicting them in your *next report*), would you change anything about how they were presented – in order to maximise their effectiveness?

For one of your reports (or a report by someone else), rewrite the main headings using the imaginative rather than generic terms, as pp. 124–5. What impact do these new headings have on your reading experience – and what impact would they have on you, if you were *writing* to these headings?

Pick up a report you are unfamiliar with, and don't know its author. Examine whether the Executive Summary (or equivalent) caters for first-time, uninformed readers such as yourself. Can you: quickly grasp its main findings, understand any technical terms or complicated sections, find further details of sections you want to know more about, etc. The report may have ideas for your next Executive Summary – and your reports should pass the same tests.

13

Securing media interest

- Identify your target media
- Pass the 'So what?' test
- Layout for press releases
- Be available to the media
- Be useful
- Vary your releases for different media
- Be a good contact
- Try using the telephone
- When your story is not covered
- Other ways to get coverage – Beyond press releases

66 'A dog bites a man' – that's a story. 'A man bites a dog'– that's a good story. 99

Jesse Lynch Williams

Identify your target media

Before you write any of your press release, think very carefully who your story is aimed at, and where and how that audience might be reached. For example, are you aiming at local small business owners, national HR managers, women with small children, teenagers keen on technology, etc.? Then look at the local/national media to see which ones reach out to your audience.

If you want ideas of which media might be interested in your story, all large newsagents stock an amazing array of magazines you may not have realised existed. Don't forget to tune into local radio stations (BBC and commercial), who have many programmes and 'slots' within programmes that specifically cover local stories. Your local library may also be worth a visit, which should have backdated copies of many magazines and newspapers.

All this might seem laborious, but it is information that you can use time and time again, and doesn't change very often. For your target media, make a record of the following: when they cover the subject of your press release, how long are their articles/programmes, who are their readers/listeners (you might have to work this out), and which journalists cover the stories.

> **Key Point:** Be warned, nothing annoys journalists more than getting press releases that are inappropriate for their publication/ radio station/audience, and the kind of story they cover. It shows you haven't looked properly at their newspaper/magazine, or listened to their radio station – and it wastes their time.

Pass the 'So what?' test

We all think our work is important, that our products and services are useful, and can make a difference – we wouldn't be in business otherwise. But it is easy to get overexcited when planning a press release. We can sometimes fail to see that, actually, our story isn't as original, different or interesting as we first thought. So before you write anything, ask yourself if it will be interesting to a 'man on the street'.

Be a really firm critique of your idea, or sleep on it before you answer! Check that people wouldn't just think, 'So what?'

> **Key Point:** The most common reasons why a press release is not picked up, say journalists, is that it is: not news, routine, too commercial, not focussed enough, too general, doesn't have a hook, and merely panders to someone's ego.

Journalists like to make links between stories – it gives their pages continuity, makes a story in itself, and encourages readers to buy the next issue or keep tuning in. So, one really effective way to get coverage for a press release is to hook (or 'piggyback' or 'link') your story to one already in the news. For example, do you have local data or a local case study to relate to a big story/issue in the national media, or can you give expert comment on the suitability of a recent government proposal?

Layout for press releases

Press releases have a pretty rigid format. Indeed, so rigid that it is as though you are completing a printed form – except of course you only start with a blank piece of paper. The web has lots of advice on their layout (and as I write, the Friends of the Earth website is particularly useful), but here are my suggested essentials:

- ◆ **Clear heading** – Give your release a clear title. Date it, or use an embargo until a given date if you want to control the timing of any media coverage.

- ◆ **Answer the 5Ws** – The who, what, when, where and why of your story, making sure you answer two or three of these in your first couple of sentences. The effect of this is that, if needed, the media should be able to cut text from the bottom of your release (right up until the first sentence) and it will still make sense/include the main content.

- ◆ **Include a quote** – Make this clear, powerful and not too long.

- ◆ **Double-space your text**, i.e. set your line spacing to 'double'.

◆ **Keep it to one side of A4** – This should be enough to summarise your story; if the media are interested and it needs more details they will contact you.

◆ **Footnotes with additional information** – Beneath the press release itself, put the name and contact details of your spokesperson, spell out any acronyms, explain any technical terms, etc.

If you think about any news story on TV, radio or in print, it presents all the key facts at the start. Their aim is tell their readers the principle details – who, what, when, where and why of the news story, or certainly answers to two or three of these – in the first couple of sentences. There are a few reasons for this, the main one being, as news aims to inform people, informing them early on is ideal. This means the audience can quickly get the main story, and then decide whether or not to continue listening/reading for more details.

This structure is represented by an upside down triangle: widest at its start (where the 5 Ws are answered), and narrower and narrower as the news story continues (with less and less new/important content).

Be available to the media

It sounds obvious, but if you put someone's name and contact details on your press release make sure they know about it, are available and that they keep their phone switched on. I have heard many stories of journalists being interested in a press release but then not able to contact the person cited on it – worse still, the contact was not fully briefed or was reluctant to talk. Your contact person/spokesperson doesn't have to be available 24/7, but they should definitely be ready and available for a few days after your press release is issued.

> **Key Point:** In advance of giving a radio interview, it's a good idea for your press release's contact person to run through their answers with someone else in the organisation/business – in particular how they will deal with any probing or difficult questions.

Be useful

People often say journalists are lazy, but in my view they are just very busy – news reporters are inundated with press releases and have to work to tight deadlines. So, if you can do something for them that will save them time, etc., you will increase the chances of your press release being used. Since you are competing with other stories for journalists' attention, here are a few ways in which you might stand out from the crowd:

◆ Make sure your release is well written, so that journalists can 'cut and paste' without editing.

◆ If your story is photogenic, can you supply a photograph to go with it, to save journalists the chore of organising their own? (Offer one, but don't send it until asked.)

◆ Can you think of a suitable headline for your story? Your heading may not be the one they finally use, but it can be a good way to catch their eye, and may even help sway them to include your story.

Vary your releases for different media

Once you have done the hard work of writing a press release you might be tempted to send it out to all your target media without altering the content. Don't. The media might be a single entity to you, but they have different readership profiles/audiences – and in many cases are competitors with one another.

In your study of the market (see above) you should have identified the audience/readership profile of various newspapers, magazines and radio stations. Use that information to help target your release to those who could be interested, and tweak your story for their particular audience.

> **Key Point:** It may take more time, but if you can make your press releases relevant and specific to each media outlet you send it to – through a specific/relevant headline, citing different geographic places and making your data relevant – it's more likely that it will be covered, and that you will be remembered in a positive light.

Be a good contact

The media rely on organisations and businesses for getting their stories – but also for getting quotes and reactions to other news. So, if you are easily contactable and can give a good interview – i.e. you are a fluent speaker and know your subject – they will make a mental note that you are useful and easy to build a rapport with, so will come back to you on other occasions. It is a reputation worth having.

Try using the telephone

People are rather glued to using email these days. But although the technology is tremendously useful I am often surprised how rarely people use the phone – even when the matter would benefit from a *conversation* rather than one-way email communication, and bearing in mind it might require a string of emails to and fro that will take longer than a phone call. Yes, journalists are humans – they won't bite; they will talk to you on the telephone.

No, don't phone them about *all* your press releases. But if, for example, you are not getting any response to your press releases, if you have a really good story for which time is pressing, or if you want to try and build a longer-term relationship with a particular media or journalist, use the good old-fashioned telephone.

When you get through, check that they have a few minutes to talk, and be prepared to maximise your time with them. It's an opportunity to find out when it is best to contact them, and how. Be polite but not overly friendly; and be prepared to talk to them about your press release, and why you think they should cover it. Also, take some notes on anything useful they feed back to you.

When your story is not covered

Your press release might be perfect, your contact person might have made themselves available, and you might even have adjusted your press release for different media, but still your story isn't covered. I am afraid that will happen – in fact, it can happen quite often. But don't think 'that was a waste of time'; your efforts are not necessarily wasted.

First, remind yourself that there may be several reasons why nobody contacted you and your story is not covered – and these could be nothing to do with the quality of your press release, nor story. For example, they might be very busy and did not have space to cover your press release (unfortunately, a far bigger story than yours may have happened); or your story might be rather similar to another one they were covering or that they covered in the previous issue (yes, the latter can influence them).

Second, comfort yourself of the gains from issuing a press release – as they may have read it even if they didn't print it. For example, if they didn't know you before they will be more likely to notice and consider your next release; and you will have reminded them of your presence and interests, etc. so they might contact you for a comment to another story.

But one thing you *shouldn't do* is to contact the media and probingly ask why they didn't use your press release. It is OK to ask them politely if your release is the sort of thing they are interested in, in particular as part of a wider discussion, but I don't advise going any further – it's intruding a bit into their job. There may be all kinds of reasons, some of which they won't remember. And, quite frankly, they will probably have more pressing work to do.

Other ways to get coverage – Beyond press releases

Press releases are the obvious and oldest way to get media coverage, but in practice there are a host of other ways to reach your audience – more imaginative, more high profile and where there may even be less competition. Here's some ideas, of three different types:

Get an immediate impact

◆ Write letters to the press

◆ Respond to radio phone-ins.

Create your own news

◆ Donate a prize for students, apprentices, or a major raffle

◆ Run a competition

◆ Do pro bono (free) work for a charity, or do something to address a local issue

◆ Mark an anniversary

◆ Fund a research study into a significant local issue/event

◆ Start/Run an awareness week.

Increase your appeal

◆ Take out an advertisement/advertorial

◆ Offer to write or feed in material for newspaper/magazine features

◆ Make a donation to a fundraising appeal

◆ Sponsor an event

◆ Become an expert

◆ Partner a larger firm in their advertising.

Further reading

Loads of good advice available on the web.

Practice writing exercises

Identify your target media as p. 130 and then collect details on when, where and how they might cover the sort of stories you would write in a press releases. Make sure you know what geographic areas these media cover, so that, when the time comes, you can write press releases that are highly specific to their audiences.

Practice writing a press release, using the format suggested in the chapter. As a subject, write an announcement about something you are pleased with (e.g. a new product, a high level/growth in sales, etc.). If necessary, make up any details.

Listen to a news bulletin. Now summarise one of the stories in just one sentence (write it, or say it out loud), making sure you cover at least three of the 5 Ws (who, what, when, where and why). This is good practice for focussing on the essentials of news stories, and hence your next press release.

Tune into the national and local news for a few days. Now, if you were writing a press release over this period, what news 'hooks' could you have used to help your release grab the media's attention?

Identify three ways to get media coverage (beyond press releases) from the list of ideas at the end of this chapter – and that you think would be feasible for your business/organisation. What are the first steps you need to take to make each of them happen?

Tidying
Your Text

Ten common grammatical and other mistakes

Less or fewer?

Singular or plural?

Beware of double negatives

Muddled words

That and which

Keep related words together

I or me?

Splitting infinitives

Apostrophes

Misuse of commas

"I don't judge people based on their race, creed, colour or gender... I judge them on their spelling, grammar, punctuation and sentence structure."
someecards.com

Each year I edit 10–15 books for publishers, and from my experience of there and elsewhere these are the most common grammatical mistakes I encounter. Keep an eye out for them.

And if you struggle with grammar, take comfort. Once you start looking into it you will discover that there are fairly fixed rules to guide you, and bit by bit you can learn the ones you need – in that way it's a bit like a science, but a very accessible one. Get yourself a reference book, look things up if you are unsure of them, and test yourself to cement your learning.

Less or fewer?

One way of classifying nouns is whether or not they can be 'counted'. Countable nouns have both a singular and a plural form, e.g. *book(s)*, *report(s)* and *desk(s)*, whereas non-countable nouns only have one form, e.g. *water*, *hope*, *air*.

When referring to a smaller quantity of any given noun, the grammatical rule is to use 'fewer' when referring to a countable noun (e.g. *fewer books, fewer reports, fewer desks*, etc.) and 'less' if the noun is non-countable (*less water, less hope, less air*, etc.).

Singular or plural?

Be careful with 'group nouns' such as *committee, government, team,* etc. that seem singular (i.e. they don't end in –s) but relate to more than one person. Do they take the singular or plural form of verbs and pronouns (*is/are, has/have, it/they*, etc.)?

Strictly speaking, a singular noun takes singular verbs and pronouns (i.e. *The committee* is *not meeting this week;* it *meets next in September / The government* has *decided* …). However, it is always best to check. For example, my Chambers reference book says: 'It is increasingly common to allow group nouns to take a plural verb in places where the group noun seems to indicate a collection of individuals rather than a single body.' (i.e. *The government* are *on holiday / The sales team* have *gone to the pub*.) Whatever view you take, be consistent within your document.

Beware of double negatives

Double negatives have two not's in the sentence, and as a result their meaning can be confusing. For example, *It is not that I'm not in support of the idea, but* … . To which one might wonder, if only for a split second, are they for or against?

Such writing can easily confuse people, so it's better and clearer to rewrite the sentence. In this case, write: *I support the idea, but* … .

Muddled words

Below are two examples of words whose meaning and usage is commonly muddled – so common that few people correct them. But if you want to write accurate English, and want your writing to impress people and sound good, it is best to be aware of these and other muddled words.

- Regularly means *on a regular basis*, i.e. every X days/weeks. It does not mean frequently, which is how some people incorrectly use it.

- Hopefully means 'with hope', e.g. *My dog looked at me hopefully*. But it is sometimes used incorrectly at the start of sentences to mean 'I hope' or 'it is hoped' (e.g. *Hopefully someone can sort this out.*) As well as being incorrect usage, it can introduce a lack of clarity – it is not always clear who is doing the hoping.

That and which

That and which are sometimes used interchangeably, but shouldn't be.

THAT introduces information *integral to the main clause* of a sentence (it is called the defining relative pronoun). In contrast, WHICH is used to introduce information that is *additional to* the main clause (it is called the non-defining relative pronoun) and is usually preceded by a comma.

In the following example 'that' introduces exactly which office Aeysha moved to:

✓ *Aeysha moved to one of the offices that had been cleaned.*

✗ *Aeysha moved to one of the offices which had been cleaned.*

And in this next example 'which' explains where I first met May, i.e. it is additional to the main clause of *May came to our offices yesterday.*

✓ *May came to our offices yesterday, which was when I first met her.*

✗ *May came to our offices yesterday which was when I first met her.*

✗ *May came to our offices yesterday, that was when I first met her.*

✓ *May came to our offices yesterday. That was when I first met her.*

Keep related words together

As a general rule, it is important to keep words together that relate to one another in terms of their ideas/thoughts – otherwise sentences can get confusing and/or introduce incorrect meanings. Here are four examples to be aware of.

The first is what is called a 'dangling participle' (or 'participle clause'), e.g. *Being in a terrible state, I was able to buy the business cheaply.*

Now, because the first phrase (*Being in a terrible state,...*) doesn't have a noun or pronoun, the reader's mind attaches the phrase's verb (being) to the first noun/pronoun (I), which follows the comma. The result is a miscommunication: the writer meant the business was in a terrible state, not I. The solution is to include a noun in the first phrase, e.g. *As the business was in a terrible state, I could buy it cheaply.*

Secondly, don't cut a subject (*our accounts* in the examples below) off from the main verb (*not seen*) by a phrase/clause that could be placed at the beginning of the sentence (*as they were late*):

- ✗ *Our accounts, as they were late, were not seen by the management group.*
- ✓ *As they were late, our accounts were not seen by the management group.*

Thirdly, put modifiers (*only*, in the example below) next to the words they relate to (*three businesses*). In this example, we need to know did they go to only three in total, or only three in Gloucester:

- ✗ They only went to *three businesses in Gloucester* (in total, or in Gloucester?)
- ✓ They only went to *three businesses* (only three in total).
- ✓ *They went to only three businesses in Gloucester* (only three in Gloucester)

And here is one final example.

- ✗ *He liked the analytical section of the report towards the end.*
- ✓ *He liked the analytical section towards the end of the report.*

I or me?

People sometimes use 'I' when they mean 'me' and vice versa. The rule is that you should use 'I' when you are the subject of the sentence, and 'me' if you are the object – and it does not matter how many other people are involved.

Still unsure? There is an easy test to work out which to use. Take this sentence: *My manager and I/me went to the meeting*. Is it *My manager and I...* or *My manager and me...*? The rule is, if you remove the other person from the sentence (*My manager and*), whether you use I/me in what is left in the sentence is what you must use in the original sentence:

✓ *My manager and I went to the meeting*

✓ *(My manager and) I went to the meeting*

✗ *(My manger and) me went to the meeting.*

Here's another example:

✓ *The taxi came to collect my colleague and me.*

✓ *The taxi came to collect (my colleague and) me.*

✗ *The taxi came to collect (my colleague and) I*

Splitting infinitives

Some people have strong views that you absolutely can't split an infinitive, i.e. putting an adverb within it, such as when the infinitive 'to go' becomes 'to boldly go...' (as in *Startrek*). However, this is usually because they were brought up on Latin, which was long regarded as the base for good English, and a Latin infinitive is only one word – it's impossible to split it!

However, language changes and this is one of the 'rules' that can occasionally be broken – occasionally. Here are two examples of when:

◆ If the adverb is closely related to the verb, then they may be best positioned together. *He lifted his hand to* gently *stroke the young animal.*

◆ Likewise, some modifiers need to be positioned next to their verb. *My job is to* really *sort out the office administration system.* (This is as per my advice in Keep related words together, above).

But be careful, there are times when splitting infinitives could result in confusion or the wrong impression. For example, the sentence *I like to in the summer get up early and go for a walk*, is rather confusing; better to write *In the summer I like to get up early and go for a walk.*

Apostrophes

Apostrophes are used EITHER to indicate possession (*Anne's book*, *Darren's report*, etc.) OR to indicate a letter is missing (*isn't*, *hadn't*, *they'll*, etc. – which are called contractions).

A bit more on the first usage. To indicate possession, an apostrophe s <'s> is added onto the end of the noun (i.e. *Robert's coat*, *Suzie's dog*, etc.). However, if the noun ends in '-s' it is now acceptable to add only the apostrophe, without the additional <s> (i.e. *James' coat*, *Jess' dog*). This prevents words ending in '-s' becoming an eye-sore (e.g. *The businesses's reaction was overwhelming.*)

Be careful of putting the apostrophe and additional <s> in the right place for the meaning, e.g. *The manager's job is to support staff* (singular), or *The managers' job is to support staff* (plural).

Be particularly careful of what are called possessive pronouns (*mine, yours, his, hers, its, ours, yours, and theirs*). Since they already indicate possession they don't need an apostrophe followed by an <s>.

NOTE: As a result, <it's> has to be substitutable by, and can only refer to, the two words <it is>.

And if you want to enjoy your next shopping trip, be alert to any green-grocer's (i.e. wrongly placed) apostrophes such as these:

- *Two video's for the price of one*
- *Tomatoes' £80p/lb*
- *Shepherds pie's, £2.50*

Misuse of commas

I can't avoid using the grammatical term 'parenthetical phrase', but all it refers to is an explanatory or qualifying word/clause inserted into a sentence, with brackets, or more commonly commas, on either side.

Both commas can be omitted if their inclusion interrupts the sentence's flow, or no pause is needed; but you cannot omit just one of the commas. For example:

✓ *The chief executive, Alan Jones, addressed the meeting after lunch.*

✓ *The chief executive Alan Jones addressed the meeting after lunch.*

✗ *The chief executive, Alan Jones addressed the meeting after lunch.*

✗ *The chief executive Alan Jones, addressed the meeting after lunch.*

✓ *Sue Arnold, who was working from home that day, was not able to attend.*

✗ *Sue Arnold, who was working from home that day was not able to attend.*

✗ *Sue Arnold who was working from home that day, was not able to attend.*

Further reading

Good Writing Guide – Ian Brooks and Duncan Marshall. Chambers Harrap Publishers, 2007.

Gwynne's Grammar – Nevile Gwynne. Ebury Press, 2013.

Improve Your Grammar – Mark Harrison, Venessa Jakeman and Ken Paterson. Palgrave Macmillan, 2012.

Improve Your Spelling – George Palmer. Routledge, 2002.

The Elements of Style – William Strunk and E B White. Longman, 2000.

www.dailywritingtips.com

Practice writing exercises

Is the familiar supermarket queue instruction, 'Five items or less', right or wrong? You will find a discussion and answer to this on the web.

Punctuate these sentences (or re-phrase them where necessary), to make their meaning absolutely clear:

◆ They only speak Welsh at home

◆ She had no earrings and make-up

◆ If your baby finds fresh fruit hard try boiling it

◆ Janet told Ruth that she had to see the doctor

◆ We stopped at the first village where there was a post office

◆ They fought with the English at Waterloo.

Edit any of these sentences as necessary. (a) The committee have decided that the team do not trust him and they never will. (b) To more than make up for it we need to really get to know the staff. (c) Being a valued customer, we would like to make you a special offer. (d) I'm not not doing that, I'll do it later.

How many different ways can you punctuate these words (you must use all of them), to create different meanings: there was no letter that day he was pleased his wife was worried.

Check that the apostrophes in these sentences are in the right position. (a) James's children played with their friends toys. (b) Susan's work isn't of other's standards. (c) Supermarket's apples are not as good this as lasts seasons'. (d) The styles' are made of stainless steel. If you have want to check your answers, or have your own teasers for me to answer, you can email me at: robert@perfecttext.org

15

Punctuation made simple

> **"**This morning I took out a comma and this afternoon I put it back in again.**"**
>
> **Oscar Wilde**

Getting punctuation right is important

People's views on punctuation differ widely. Some people have very strong opinions on its usage, but others are more relaxed. And some people use a lot of punctuation in their writing, whereas others use a lot less. Either way, punctuation can totally alter the meaning of a sentence, so you need to get on top of it. For example:

> *The judge said the convict is mad. / 'The judge', said the convict, 'is mad'.*
> *'Let's eat, Grandpa.' / 'Let's eat Grandpa.'*

The purpose of punctuation

Punctuation was invented by the Greeks to inform their actors when they should breathe – as Lynne Truss reminds us in her highly enter-taining book on punctuation (*Eats, Shoots and Leaves*), which is most definitely worth a read.

> **Key Point:** If you are unsure where to put your punctuation, try reading your text out loud, *without any punctuation*, and you should realise what punctuation is needed from the pauses you naturally take. (Today, punctuation is orientated towards grammar rather than oral speech, but this technique provides a very useful guide.)

Different types of punctuation produce different length pauses, as summarised in this poem by Cecil Hartley (1818), published in his book *Principles of Punctuation: Or, The Art of Pointing:*

> The stops point out, with truth, the time of pause
> A sentence doth require at ev'ry clause.
> At ev'ry comma, stop while *one* you count;
> At semicolon, *two* is the amount;
> A colon doth require the time of *three*;
> The period *four*, as learned men agree.

Get it? Commas insert the shortest pause, then semi-colons followed by colons (but neither of these are that common so don't worry about them too much), and finally the full stop.

NOTE: Dashes and brackets weren't mentioned here; they come, in that order, between commas and semi-colons. Nor were question marks and exclamation marks, which come after full stops.

Punctuation can be personal

As I said above, people's usage of and views on commas can vary widely – which must be annoying for people learning English! In fact, when I gave a training course to a high-street retailer they told me they spent *ages* (their emphasis) deciding about the position of commas.

How is that possible? Well, more commas doesn't necessarily prevent something from being *understood*. And secondly, where commas occur is only partly about grammatical rules; *around 30 per cent is down to the writer's choice* (according to Lynne Truss' book mentioned above). So, some commas are neither right nor wrong, they are just the author's choice.

People also use other punctuation differently. Some use semi-colons where others might prefer a comma or full-stop. Academics tend to use colons, which few other people do. And some people like dashes – and even use them too much, and incorrectly – whereas others use a comma instead.

Correct uses of commas

All English grammar books contain guidance on the usage of commas, but they use technical language and often run to several pages. So, I have come up with something easier to understand, shorter and more practical – being centred on whether their usage is optional or compulsory.

You can download the one-page table from my website's blog (www. perfecttext.org/unsure-of-your-commas/), but what I view as the five compulsory uses of commas is given below <with the technical terms in these angular brackets for those who want them>.

Compulsory commas, 1 of 5 – in lists of items

◆ **Where more than one item** – *We have national, regional, local and area-specific teams*. NOTE: use semi-colons where the items are complex/contain several words, e.g. *We have fresh home-made bread and cheese; soup; potato and chive salad with an onion dressing; and roast vegetable and fennel flan*.

◆ **Where several adjectives (colours, size, location, descriptions, etc.) are together** – *He was tall, dark and handsome*. NOTE: don't use a comma if the adjectives are conveying a single idea, e.g. *She wore shiny red shoes*.

Compulsory commas, 2 of 5 – when adding information to a sentence

◆ **Information within a sentence** – Put commas either side of the information, e.g. *The sales team, who work from home, don't need a desk*. <This is a clause within a clause, what are called bracketing commas.>

◆ **Information at the end of a sentence** – Put a comma before this, e.g. *Double-entry bookkeeping is a form of accounting, which is taught at the local college*. NOTE: With the comma it means <u>accounting</u> is taught at the college, but without it <u>double-entry bookkeeping</u> is taught at the college (although strictly speaking the 'which' should then be 'that'). <Non-defining relative clauses.>

Compulsory commas, 3 of 5 – when using 'joining words' <conjunctions>

◆ **Before joining words (and, but, etc.) when the sentence is long or complicated/the subject changes** – *Our business is expanding into European markets early next year, and in February we are also introducing a new accounting system. / He is arriving later, but we will go out beforehand.* [Yes, we were all taught commas are not needed before conjunctions, but that was for short, simple sentences we wrote when we were young.]

Compulsory commas, 4 of 5 – where a pause seems natural

◆ **To separate sentences with two parts (one part is often identifiable by an –ing word)** – *Having left, he missed the Chairman's conclusions.* Or, *You cannot go home, it would leave nobody in the office.* <These –ing words are present participles.>

◆ **Where one part of a sentence (identifiable by if ..., unless ..., although ..., however, etc.) depends on the other** – *If you get stuck, give me a call.* NOTE: the comma is often not needed if the sentence is expressed the other way (unless the sentence is very long): *Give me a call if you get stuck.* <Main and <u>subordinate clause</u>.>

◆ **When introductory words (however, in addition, therefore, instead, etc.) are mid-sentence** – in these situations put commas on either side, e.g. *After he left the business, however, the company performed better.* Or you can have a semi-colon before and a comma afterwards, e.g. *They are busy today; however, they can see you tomorrow.*

Compulsory commas, 5 of 5 – to clarify what you mean

◆ **To avoid misunderstandings** – the inclusion or not of a comma can determine a sentence's meaning, e.g. *Outside the office staff were assembling* is not clear, whereas these two formats are: *Outside, the office staff were assembling,* and *Outside the office, staff were assembling.*

Above all else, be consistent

The position/inclusion of some punctuation is a matter of choice. What matters (and what readers usually notice) is not what you do, but that you are consistent across your text. The following are examples of the main areas where punctuation varies, so take a stand and stick to it:

◆ Quoted speech can be introduced with a comma, colon or neither.

◆ Quote marks can be single (') or double (")

◆ Punctuation can go inside or outside quote marks, and some people vary this according to whether the quote is a full sentence (inside) or not (outside).

◆ A comma can be placed before the 'and' in a list of items (what is called the Oxford/Serial comma e.g. *He came with a bat, ball, and glove.*)

◆ People adopt different conventions, for example, as to how abbreviations are written (e.g. or eg and etc. or etc), and what to put at the end of numbered/bulleted lists of items (nothing, semi-colons or full-stops).

Colons

Some people get muddled between colons and semi-colons. Well, they have their similarities – both occur midway through a sentence – but they should be used in very different places.

The main usage of colons (see below for steers on semi-colons) is where you want to explain or give an example(s) of something you have just written. They can be 'translated' into the words *namely/that is to say*, i.e. they expand on the first part of the sentence. For example: *The business has had its best year ever: profits are up 45%*. Note that, in this usage of colons, either side of the colon is dependent on the other, which is not the case for semi-colons.

Other uses of colons are: in ratios (2:1), in some film/book titles (e.g. *Business Writing Skills: Everything you need to know*), and to introduce long quotations and (sometimes) lists and direct speech.

Colons can also be used to introduce something you want to emphasise. For example: *Our research shows one thing above all: people like people*. Or, *Always remember this about housewives: they're our customers*.

Semi-colons

The main usage of semi-colons is instead of full-stops; they connect two clauses that are so connected that there is no need for a full-stop, but a comma would provide too short a break (as in this sentence). They can be 'translated' into the words *and/but*.

Other uses are: instead of commas in lists of items, and where one or more items take several words to describe. And if you are using *nevertheless*, *furthermore* or *moreover* midway through a sentence, you will need a semi-colon before them, in order to provide a longish pause. For example, *It has been a great financial year; moreover, sales forecasts for next year look very strong.*

Commas, dashes and brackets

If you have something that is *additional* to a sentence's main meaning, you have what is called a parenthetical phrase ('an explanatory or qualifying word, clause or sentence in a wider passage of text'). Here, you have the choice of using commas, dashes or brackets/parentheses. So when should you use which?

As demonstrated below, the 'break' provided by these three types of punctuation increases as you move from commas (the shortest), to dashes (which also emphasise the phrase within them) and brackets (used when the content is less relevant to the rest of sentence). Note that in each case you can delete the parenthetical phrase and the sentence still makes sense.

- ◆ **Commas**: *James, who used to run his own business, became the company MD.*

- ◆ **Dashes**: *He arrived late for the meeting – nothing unusual there – and so couldn't make his presentation.*

- ◆ **Brackets**: *Helen's report to the meeting (see attached) summarised the company's situation perfectly.*

The other main use of dashes is at the end of sentences, where what follows is an aside to what preceded it, or represents a change of thought. For example, *Let's call up Helen from Accounts – she is always good at sorting things out.*

Brackets/parentheses are also commonly usually used for references, e.g. giving the years someone was born/died, reference details, etc.

Quote marks

Quote marks can be single (') or double ("). In the UK we tend to use single quotes, with double quotes for quotes within quotes; however, the opposite way around is also permissible – what matters is consistency within a document.

Quote marks may be used in the following situations:

◆ Directly quoted speech – *'Wake up', said Muriel.*

◆ Short extracts of another document (but no need for quote marks when it is a longer, indented extract).

◆ A different meaning for a word than normal – *Can we get some 'spice' into the report?*

◆ The word's usage is slightly out of place, e.g. when using humour or irony, the word is rather technical or less formal language than what surrounds it, etc. – *The marketing department are like 'ice'.*

◆ A summary of what someone else said, but in your own words – *The CEO thinks our prospects are 'pretty good'.*

Hyphenated words

Hyphens can be one of the hardest things to get right – for three reasons. There are a lot of rules about when and when not to use them; sometimes their usage is optional (or going through a period of change in our language); and many people make mistakes, which results in confusion as to what is right/wrong.

Here's my guidance as to whether hyphens are needed, optional or not needed.

Where hyphens are NEEDED

◆ When the word has a prefix (*non-related, pre-meeting*), would result in a repeat of a vowel (*anti-ideas, re-establish*) or before a date or name (*pre-1900*).

◆ When two nouns combine to form a verb (*A spot check* → *To spot-check*)

◆ When a noun and adjective/participle combine into a word (*long-lasting, computer-mad/decision-making, customer-orientated*)

◆ When there is an adjective and noun in one word (*high-energy, red-haired*)

◆ When there is a noun/adjective together with a participle (*money-saving/long-lasting*)

◆ In a phrase made into a noun (*There was a build-up of traffic. Or, there was a break-in last night*)

◆ To avoid confusion (*re-cover, re-create, re-mark*)

◆ And more familiar uses: numbers between 21 and 99 (*thirty-six*); numbers combined with words (*18-year-old boys, 5-minute break*); words starting in self- (*self-improvement*); and fractions (*one-fifth*).

Where hyphens are OPTIONAL

'Compound nouns' involve the fusion of two or more nouns into a single word; they start out hyphenated but gradually evolve into a single word.

◆ *play group* → *play-group* → *playgroup*

◆ *lamp shade* → *lamp-shade* → *lampshade*

◆ *back office* → *back-office* OR *backoffice*

◆ *pre war* → *pre-war* OR *prewar.*

Also, when a prefix ends in a vowel and so does the following word. Here, a hyphen is becoming less common, with single words gradually replacing many, e.g. *Pre-arrange* OR *prearrange, co-operate* OR *cooperate*

Where hyphens are NOT NEEDED

◆ In phrasal verbs (which are made up of a main verb and an adverb or preposition) e.g. *You should build up some credit,*

NOT *'build-up'*. Or, *Why not break in if you have no key*, NOT *'break-in'*. (NOTE: These are different from the nouns, above.)

◆ Adverbs ending in –ly followed by an adjective (*It is a badly written report*, NOT *'badly-written'*. Or, *An easily found office*, NOT *'easily-found'*.

However

When using words such as *however, consequently, as a result* and *moreover*, it is not compulsory to have a comma when they appear *at the start of a sentence* – it can depend on the flow of the sentence – but it is thought necessary to have commas on either side when they appear *mid-sentence* (or use a semi-colon before them and a comma afterwards). These examples should demonstrate:

◆ *However, please feel free to contact us if you are not satisfied.*

◆ *As a result we have decided to reimburse you.*

◆ *In November, sales slumped; moreover, they were lower than our worst forecast.*

◆ *The managing director is not here this week; consequently, we will have to delay resolution of the matter.*

Further reading

Eats, Shoots and Leaves – Lynne Truss. Profile Books, 2003.

Improve Your Punctuation – Graham King. Harper Collins, 2009.

Perfect Punctuation – Stephen Curtis. Random House Books, 2007.

Perfect Text blog. Available at: www.perfecttext.org/blog/

www.dailywritingtips.com

Practice writing exercises

Remove the punctuation from a passage of text (100–300 words). Now read it out loud, noticing where you naturally pause, and for how long. This is a good way of working out where and what punctuation is needed in any text. Your chosen punctuation should be close to what is in the original, but it may not match it precisely because, as discussed in this chapter, people's use of some punctuation can vary.

These three sentences can be punctuated in different ways, to give different meanings. What are they? (a) My neighbour swore I went to the clifftop for a walk. (b) Henry said his mother should leave before the traffic built up. (c) Raj thought Shabnam wasn't good at the job.

And now a longer text. This one can be punctuated in two different ways to give two very different meanings. See if you can spot them: 'Dear John I want a man who knows what love is all about you are generous kind thoughtful people who are not like you admit to being useless and inferior you have ruined me for other men I yearn for you I have no feelings whatever when we're apart I can be forever happy will you let me be yours Gloria.'

Write three sentences using each of the following: (a) colons, (b) semi-colons, (c) brackets, (d) dashes. If you want to check your answers, you can email me at: robert@perfecttext.org.

16

BEFORE you press 'Print' (How to edit and proofread)

66 With all editing ... I react sulkily at first, but then I settle down and get on with it, and a year later I have my book in my hand. 99

Michael Morpurgo

When you have done all the hard work of *writing* something, it is tempting to rush to get it sent out, printed, posted on the web, etc. – which would mean skipping what are the essential final stages of any writing job: editing and proofreading.

As I have said elsewhere, don't underestimate the time involved for these, and don't beat yourself up if it takes a long time. I often tell people that, together, editing and proofreading will take 25–40% of the total time working on a job.

The terms 'editing' and 'proofreading' are sometimes used inter-changeably by businesses, but to the publishing world they are distinct activities with different purposes, methods and results. This chapter explores them both, starting with editing.

> **Key Point:** MS Word's 'Spelling & Grammar' checker (on the Review tab) has scope for highlighting not just spelling and grammatical mistakes but also unusual and less acceptable writing styles, e.g. flagging up the presence of clichés, passive sentences, gender-specific words, etc. You will find an endless list of things you can choose it to highlight tucked away here: File > Options > Proofing > Settings.

Editing defined and explained

Editing is done before a document is laid out, and is concerned with broad issues such as: checking whether a document achieves its objectives and whether there is balance and flow between sections; applying the house style (if there is one); improving the phrasing of any sentences to make them clearer; consulting with the author over any queries, etc. Editing can therefore involve making some quite large changes; and checking for factual accuracies etc. can take quite a while.

A structural edit

In order to review a document's overall structure, content and flow, etc., I find it best to do a 'structural edit' first. To do this I look at a printed version rather than one on screen – that way I give it more attention. And, very importantly, I read it *without a pencil/biro in my hand*, for as soon as I have one I get drawn into making the changes associated with *detailed* editing or proofreading. As I read, I make a mental note of the larger changes that are needed.

If you prefer, have a pencil/biro in your hand but only allow yourself to write *on a separate piece of paper* from the text, and only write your assessment of the *major* issues – rather than detailed corrections, which can be done in a second edit. (Sometimes I circle things on the original text, but only so that I know what needs addressing later.)

Only edit when you are feeling strong

Some editing jobs take a lot of time, and can become confusing and even disheartening. For example, it may require moving endless slabs of text around, deleting what you spent ages working on, getting muddled about the changes you are making, and worrying if you are making the text better … or not.

So if you are doing a major edit like this, my view is you need to be feeling strong. You need to have the time to work through all the edits, confident that they are for the better, and to have the perseverance to get to the end. It is not a job for when you are feeling a little bit 'down', tired or last thing at night. And don't give up half way through: if you thought the changes would make your text better, they probably will … you just need to get there.

Editing takes time and effort – think positively

Clients of mine sometimes express surprise and frustration that their editing takes them so *long* – and be warned, it can. However, I remind them to think that each time they make improvements their document is becoming much better.

If you talk to any full-time writer – such as an author, copywriter or journalist – they will tell you that it is not abnormal for a document to go through three or four drafts, with quite significant changes in between.

Use an A–Z list

When doing more detailed editing, and when proofreading, it's a good idea to keep a record of the document's unusual or preferred spellings on an A–Z grid beside you, for you to refer back to when needed.

This is especially useful when editing/proofreading long documents, or where you take long breaks in-between sessions and might not remember an unusual word or preferred spelling from earlier in the document. And if you are working with publishers or typesetters (who lay documents out for publication) they may ask to see such details, so they know the spellings you have adopted and can make global changes (or undo yours) if needed.

Proofreading defined and explained

Proofreading is best done *once the document has been laid out for publication* or is virtually finished. It is about checking finer details such as the page layout and numbering, consistency of headings and spellings, etc. It may also involve correcting anything missed during editing. Ideally it is restricted to only making changes that are absolutely necessary (e.g. misspellings, wrong punctuation, insert/delete spaces) – otherwise they could impact on the document's layout, which would require it to be re-typeset and the proofreading process started again. Proofreading should therefore take less time, and involve smaller and fewer changes.

Wear a different 'hat' for proofreading

Proofreading cannot be done the way one normally reads; it requires having a very different mindset and wearing a different 'hat'. Let me explain.

When reading a document, our objective is to *understand*, which we can do even if it contains small mistakes such as typos, wrong punctuation, inconsistent formatting, etc., – and even if we skim read. In fact, we don't always notice misspellings (some of us are better at spotting them than others) because our eyes recognise and digest words from their *shape* rather than having to read each letter or sound, one by one. We can also be unaware of many minor details on the page (e.g the headers and footers), and not see inconsistencies (e.g. the formatting applied to sub-headings).

But proofreading is concerned with *checking* as well as understanding, which requires us to do a different kind of 'reading'. It means a type of reading that *does* check word spellings, watches for any inconsistencies, and looks at the fine details.

In summary, proofreading can't be done quickly – in fact, you should be forcing yourself to slow down.

Proof correction marks

If you are proofreading on paper (i.e. a 'hard copy') it is worth deciding beforehand *how* you are going to mark your corrections – i.e. are you going to use any symbols or shorthand? That might sound strange, and an overkill for your needs, but using signs will make you faster and happier in your work. Hear me out.

Take a look at the BSI's proof correction marks (you can download them from the website, bsigroup.co.uk) or one of the similar versions available on the web. Don't be thrown by how many marks there are; you will only need a few, and many of them are common sense and therefore easy – and quite fun – to learn. From my experience, however, using the signs can be a faster way of working because they mean I don't have to write words and instructions in the margins as I proofread, and I don't have to decipher notes and scribbles when making the changes onto a file. The symbols convey the same meaning to everyone, instantly. Give them a try.

Also, proofreading isn't the most exciting of tasks, so you might as well enjoy yourself along the way – and the marks are about as close to writing Ancient Egyptian as any of us will ever get.

Maximise your effort

You have to check absolutely everything when proofreading – yes, absolutely everything – and you will be better at spotting errors if you do the following:

- **Improve your knowledge** – Brush up on your knowledge of punctuation, grammar and spelling, so that you are confident about what is right and what is wrong. Better still, make a list of things you sometimes get wrong as a reminder of things to keep an eye out for.

- **Check more closely** – Do anything to increase your awareness as you read. For example, leave it for a while beforehand and only do it when you are feeling alert; move a pen or your finger over each word, to ensure you focus your eyes and don't skip ahead; use a ruler under each line as you read; print it in a different font, with different page breaks; read it out loud; and finally read it backwards, which is a great (but slower) way to check your spelling – and you can read each sentence forwards afterwards, to make sure it makes sense.

- **Focus where mistakes are most likely** – Most of a document's text will have been checked several times by its author, and the editor, whereas other details may be newer, and only glanced over or not checked at all. So, check carefully any 'rich content', i.e. that has a lot of details (e.g. tables, figures and references); where content is easily overlooked (captions, the start and end of each page, and in overly familiar information such as people's names and contact details); and also any awkward content (unusual names and spellings, long words, etc.).

Watch out! Watch out!

Proofreading is particularly hard in these situations: when checking a long document (because we can lose concentration); when in a hurry (we may skip over things, and don't read carefully enough); and when proofreading our own work (the words are so familiar to us that we see/read what we think/want to be there rather than checking what is actually written on the page).

In addition to the ideas under 'Check more closely' (above), these techniques should also help:

◆ Scan the text first, to see what sort of things to look out for in particular.

◆ Proofread in a structured/methodical way, e.g. first checking all tables, then all the headings … and finally the text.

◆ Keep a checklist of unusual words and choices of spellings in an A–Z grid, which you can refer back to as needed.

◆ Make a note of the layout and formatting of any items that are repeated but don't appear together (e.g. headings, tables, headers and footers, references), to ensure they are consistent across the document.

◆ Take regular breaks.

Common errors

As a recap to this chapter, the following are the most common formatting errors that I encounter when copy-editing and proofreading. In some cases I propose what are fairly widely followed 'rules', but in other cases what really matters is consistency across your document.

◆ 1980s not 1980's – the latter used to be common practice, but has largely been dropped.

◆ MPs not MP's – the latter used to be common practice, but has largely been dropped.

◆ Abbreviations and contractions – the former should have a full stop at the end to indicate letters are missing (e.g., etc., ref.); whereas contractions don't, because the first and last letter are present (Dr, Mr, Mrs, St).

◆ Capitalisation – when referring to a specific Figure 4, or Chapter 3, use capitals.

◆ Dates – in the UK the normal format is 25 December 2014, with no commas (US style is different: December 25, 2014).

◆ Dashes – they might all look the same, but there are three different sorts, with different lengths and meanings. A hyphen is the shortest (-), and is used between words (e.g. fast-food outlet). An 'en rule' is longer – it has a gap on either side, like here – and is used to isolate a phrase. It is also used to indicate equal weight to two words, e.g. north–south divide and Anglo–German relations. 'Em rules' are longer still, which are used e.g. to mark an interruption within direct speech. (They are called en and em rules because they are the width of the letters 'n' and 'm' in the given typeface.)

◆ Indenting – the first line of paragraphs is often indented in longer documents and books (especially fiction), but even in that house style no indenting should be given to the first paragraph of a chapter, nor after a sub-heading, image, table, figure nor quote.

◆ -ise/ize – many people don't realise but -ize is now accepted in the UK (as well as in the US), i.e. organization, realize, recognize, etc. However, be careful of words ending in -ise, many of which *always take –ise*, even when in the US/using US spellings (e.g. advertise, advise, enterprise, etc).

◆ Lists – in an indented list of short items, there is no need for punctuation at the end of each item, apart from a full stop at the end of the list. If the items are longer, put a semi-colon at the end of each item; and if the items are full sentences or two or more lines, use full stops at the end of each one.

◆ Percentages – it is normal practice to use the words per cent (not percent, which is US style), and only use % in tables. However, house style can overrule this; what matters is consistency.

◆ Position of punctuation – in the UK, punctuation normally

goes *inside* quote marks, but sometimes only if it is a complete sentence; and they go *outside* the quote marks if it is an incomplete quote.

◆ Quote marks – practice varies, but much UK writing uses single quote marks, and double marks within single marks if there is a quote within a quote.

◆ Titles – use italics for titles of books, films, newspapers, TV programmes and journals (e.g. *Animal Farm*, the *Daily Telegraph*, *Doctor Who*, etc.).

◆ Word confusions – don't confuse words such as effect/affect, compliment/complement, practice/practise, licence/license, etc.

◆ US spellings – this won't affect everyone, but if you are working in the US or have US parent companies etc., remember the US's different spellings extend beyond ize/yze. Apply these examples to similar spelled words (US spelling first): color not colour; judgment not judgement; traveling not travelling; center not centre; defense not defence; fulfill not fulfil; percent not per cent; maneuver not manoeuvre; etc.

Further reading

How to Write – Alastair Fowler. OUP, 2006

Oxford Guide to Plain English – Martin Cutts. OUP, 2009.

Practice writing exercises

Take a piece of text from a newspaper, magazine or somewhere else – one of around 300–800 words. Using a highlighter pen, identify the main points, so that you reduce its length by around 50 per cent. This should make you familiar with doing more significant editing, and show you that such reductions are always possible if you need to – but it can be painful to see all those other words deleted!

Read the following text *without* pausing.

> The human mnid deos not raed ervey leter by istlef, but the wrod
> as a wlohe. The oredr of the ltteers in the wrod can be in a total
> mses but you can sitll raed it wouthit any porbelm.

The passage shows how fast we can read text, and how easy it is to understand, even when there are lots of typos. Now clearly you would never have to check a text with as many errors as this, but the exercise shows that, to do effective proofreading, we need to do *more than understand*. To proofread, we need to really slow down, so that we are *checking* as well as reading and understanding.

Pick up three or four very different kinds of books, e.g. fiction and non-fiction, and examine the styles that each one adopts for some of the list of items at the end of this chapter. Any differences between them (e.g. the use of -ise/ize and quote marks, the position of punctuation, etc.) show you that, while there are conventions, publishers adopt their own styles – and to some degree you can too.

Take a look at BSI's proof correction marks, or others available on the web. Learn the marks that you are most likely to use when editing (e.g. delete and insert; change regular text to bold or italic, and vice versa; change lower case to upper case, and vice versa; etc.). Try to start using these symbols when you edit.

Part **6**

Final Reminders

17

Watch out! Watch out!

You need a plan for your writing

... and a target word length

Make sure you know your readers

Don't just 'cut and paste'

When you are stuck, take a break

Do a proper edit

Ask someone else to look at your work

Don't proofread on screen

Don't proofread your own work

And finally ... don't rush the final stages

To end my book here are a few important reminders for any writing job – important writing principles that we all ignore at times, for example in an effort to save time and money, *but shouldn't*. I hope they will put you straight, and get your writing back on track.

You need a plan for your writing

Be careful; if you write without a plan you might have to do a lot of editing later – and more than should have been necessary. Your plan doesn't need to be that detailed, you just need to organise your thoughts a little before you start writing, so that your text flows between paragraphs, and you give the right balance between the different things you want to say.

... and a target word length

Without a word length you have no discipline as you write, and won't properly assess whether or not given words and phrases should be included. Remember, writing *more* text isn't necessarily better – for most outputs, it is now generally recognised that 'less is more'.

Make sure you know your readers

If you don't know (or haven't thought about) *who* you are writing for, and *where* your document/text is going to be read, you are at risk of writing something from the wrong angle. Different types of readers look for different things, and how they see and read it varies between places (web/magazine/brochures). You need to take these into account in your writing.

Don't just 'cut and paste'

It might sometimes seem quicker to just cut and paste, but watch out ... make sure the text you are copying is written, structured and phrased from the perspective that you want in your *new document*. Unfortunately, invariably it won't be written in quite the right way. Tedious, I know, but better to start writing from scratch.

When you are stuck, take a break

If you get stuck it's best to move onto writing something else – or take a break completely and come back to it later. Working at it again and again won't solve things. Recognise that we all get stuck sometimes, and struggle to find the right words. You will quickly sort it out later, if you approach it with a fresh mind/pair of eyes.

Do a proper edit

The final stage of writing anything is proofreading, which involves correcting any typos, inconsistencies and any problems with the document's layout, etc. But before you proofread you should do an edit, which involves deciding about larger issues such as does your document do what you want it to, does the text flow, and is the overall balance of the document right, etc. Don't skip this stage, as you will be unlikely to notice these points when you focus on the fine details of proofreading.

Ask someone else to look at your work

Writing is done alone – it has to be. But the lack of exposure to others' views means we can get overly attached to (and proud of) what we have written. Indeed, it might seem preferable *not* to ask for feedback before going to print, in case any of it is critical of our work. However, if you choose carefully *who* you ask – someone who will do a thorough and objective job, and to whom you explain what you are writing, and any areas you particularly want comments – your document will almost certainly benefit from a second pair of eyes.

Don't proofread on screen

Proofreading is more than reading; it is about *checking*. And somehow, when a document is printed out in front of us, it heightens our critical attention, so we are more likely to spot any errors. In contrast, if you try and check a document on screen, after having written and edited it there as well, you won't see it with the fresh eye that you need to.

Don't proofread your own work

Another proofing error to the above is thinking you can spot your own errors. But when you are very familiar with the words, you will read them for what you had *meant to say* rather than checking what is written in front of you. And as you very are familiar with the text you will speed ahead, and not check properly. So, to do a *proper proofread*, give your work to someone else to check. Or at the very least leave it for a day or two so that when you come to proofread it you are reading it afresh.

And finally ... don't rush the final stages

As you get near the end of a writing job it can be tempting to rush or omit the final stages of editing and proofreading. But, no matter how rushed for time you are, be careful. Although it is lovely to *complete* something – to put it to bed and see your work in print – it will nearly always benefit from a final check, which you won't do if you rush. At the very least, leave it overnight, or a day or two, and then come back to it.

That's it from me. Enjoy your writing, keep at it, and good luck with everything.

33534874R00107

Printed in Great Britain
by Amazon